Testimonials and Reviews

"How to start a successful meeting—use humor! Henry Haverstock lies awake nights polishing his one-liners to kick off our Y's Men weekly meetings. He helps make our meetings fun to come to, which is the success of any Club. It's high time he shared this collection of humor with the world."

—Walter S. Carpenter, President,
Metro Y's Men Club, Minneapolis

"For 28 years, Henry Haverstock's gift of humor has brightened our meetings. Henry's one-liners have always given us a warm chuckle and a moment of lightheartedness."

—Richard England, President,
Exchange Club of Downtown Minneapolis

"All 110 members of our Rotary Club would agree with me that our weekly meetings and service projects just wouldn't be as much fun if it weren't for Henry and his one-liners. Since I've started to repeat his jokes, more and more people are coming around me. They don't want to be with me, they just walk around me. I can assure you that to have Henry's collected jokes in one volume makes for one of those very special and rare books."

—Jim Ullyot, President,
Minneapolis City of Lakes Rotary Club

"This book is a day brightener for anyone, and is a must for any public speaker."

—Bob Minish, Secretary,
Minneapolis City of Lakes Rotary Club

Henry's put them all together here
From his copious humor files;
One-liners for every occasion,
To produce laughs, chuckles and smiles.

—George O. Ludcke, advertising executive
in Minneapolis, and for years a frequent
contributor of limericks in the above style to the
Wall Street Journal's "Salt and Pepper" column

"I spent all night turning the pages and laughing my way through the book. Someday I hope to read it."

—Groucho Marx

by Henry W. Haverstock

A Robert Parker & Associates Book

HENRY'S HILARIOUS ONELINERS
by Henry W. Haverstock

Cover Art and Illustrations by Barry Lawrence

Text Design & Book Development by
Robert Parker & Associates
and Laser Set of Minnetonka

First Printing, May, 1991, Soft Cover
First Printing, this edition, August, 1991
ISBN 1-879916-03-7
Library of Congress Catalog Card Number 91-90330

Dedication

To All Those People Who Love To Laugh

**Ladies and Gentleman,
Children of All Ages...**

Welcome to fun and humor by my close friend and associate, and namesake, Henry my man.

As The One and Only LAUGHING MOUSE, I , Henry of Hopkins, seek nothing more than for you to be joyful and happy. And from time to time when you find it in your heart to leave a little cheese around, I would be most appreciative.

The material contained in this book has been collected over many years from a variety of sources, often passed on to me by my associates, to be used in my various talks before clubs and business dinners. Many of the original authors are unknown, and some one-liners have been attributed to more than one author. Therefore, it is truly impossible to list each source. I would like for this to be an acknowledgment of appreciation to the authors for the thoughts, if not the words, of witticism contained herein.

Henry W. Haverstock

Acknowledgments

This book would not be complete without acknowledging the debt of gratitude owed to those who egged me on in my sallies at humor and/or held their noses in polite—if occasionally ribald—forbearance on those occasions when a one-liner fell flat in the telling. Over the years I have tested my one-liners before a number of groups, including my City of Lakes Rotary Club, The Minneapolis Downtown Exchange Club and The Metro Y's Men's Club, among others. It's interesting that the very same one-liner when told to one group, will "fall flat," and when told to another will bring gales of laughter.

In addition to acknowledging my debt of gratitude to these groups, I want to thank certain individuals for their help and encouragement in various ways: the members of my own family including my wife Shirley and my children, my long-time Rotary friend Jim Ullyot for his encouragement and the preliminary review of most of the one-liners and the occasional elimination of duplications; And friends who suggested one-liners including fellow Rotarians Bob Minish, Gus Swanson and Jim Ullyot, Exchangites Carl Johnson and Stan Stanz and Y's Man Bob Wilcox; And other supportive people including J. Kenneth DeWerff, Robert Holtze, Fred Lange and Al Johnson.

Henry W. Haverstock

Introduction

Laughter is good for the spirit. Laughter promotes good health. The late Norman Cousins, in his book *Anatomy of an Illness*, showed how laughter in his own life helped him survive a near-fatal disability and extended his life for many years.

Increasingly, laughter is recognized as an essential element to a balanced life. In recognition of this, a new TV channel was recently set up for cable TV, devoted exclusively to funny, laugh-producing programming.

People seek out friends who can enjoy a good laugh, particularly when the laugh is on them. President Ronald Reagan was a master at that kind of good natured humor. He reportedly once denied, for example, that his hair was gray, and alleged that it was only prematurely orange.

For many years—and without any particular system about it—I have enjoyed collecting what I considered funny one-liners. Some time ago, I decided to bring these random bits and pieces together into one volume. At the same time, I have been testing these one-liners before various groups in which I am active, including Rotary, Minneapolis Downtown Exchange Club, the Y's Men's clubs and others. I am happy to report that they usually bring a good laugh, though sometimes only a good natured groan—or, on rare occasion, hisses or boos.

As a practicing lawyer in Minneapolis, I have even included—and I especially enjoy—some, but not all, of the many jokes aimed at my own profession.

My collection of one-liners, to which I am constantly adding, covers a broad range of subjects. Since they have come to me in no particular order, I have chosen to present them in that same way here: spontaneous, unpredictable and in no particular sequential order. I always try to avoid off-color jokes or jokes that I consider to be in poor taste.

Very little of my humor is original but much of it has undergone re-wording. This is due in large part to my inability to write as fast as the stories are told oratorically. With the printed word, this has not, of course, presented the same problem. I must say, however, that I have encountered a number of joke books where I could not find more than one or two one-liners I considered to be funny. This could be more a matter of deficiency on my part than on that of the authors of those volumes.

In any case, it will be for you, the reader, to determine whether my choice of one-liners produces for you, health-giving laughter. Since one-liners are short and generally easy to remember, I hope that you can use some of them to add interest and sparkle to all of your own social encounters.

Have fun.

Henry W. Haverstock
Minneapolis
March, 1991

1. Witness on stand to the presiding judge: "I swore to tell the truth but every time I try, some lawyer objects."

2. A man is crying his head off at the funeral of the town's richest citizen. He is asked if he is a relative and replies: "No, that's why I'm crying."

3. A sensible girl is not so sensible as she looks because a sensible girl has more sense than to look sensible.

4. Newspaper retraction: "Last week we noted that Mr. Jones was a defective in the police force. This was a typographic error. Mr. Jones is really a detective in the police farce."

5. An ad in a Connecticut newspaper: "Lost—one upper dental plate by an alumnus in the vicinity of Psi Upsilon. Finder return to Psi U asth thoon asth pothible."

6. A man went to jail for making big money— about one inch too big.

7. They've developed a new insecticide that doesn't actually kill flies but makes them so sexy that you can swat them two at a time.

8. He's the sort of fellow who can go into an empty room and blend right in.

9. The population of Blackduck, Minnesota, stays about even. Every time a baby is born, someone leaves town.

10. A couple had a disagreement: She wanted a formal church wedding and he didn't want to get married.

11. A speaker apologized for being late. He said he stopped on the way for confession and got caught behind a used car salesman.

12. A man went on an elephant hunt but had to turn back. He developed a hernia carrying the decoy.

13. About the time a man is cured of swearing, it's time to make out another income tax return.

14. Mae West: "Too much of a good thing can be wonderful."

15. Unsolicited endorsement of a medicine: "My wife was at death's door and one bottle of your medicine pulled her through."

16. Husband, about his wife: "She talks about 100 words a minute with gusts to 200."

17. An employer told his friend that he was looking for a cashier. The friend replied: "I thought you just hired one." The employer said: "I did. That's the one I'm looking for."

18. Alexander Graham Bell Polaski was the first telephone pole.

19. A dentist had a patient whose breath was so bad that he had to work on his teeth through his ear.

20. A wife told her husband that the car had water in the battery. The husband asked: "Where is the car?" She replied innocently: "It's in the swimming pool."

21. A man's brother claimed to be a vegetarian. He explained that he ran the vegetables through the cow and then ate the cow.

22. Teacher to student: "What was the former Russian leader called?" Tsar. "His wife?" Tsarina. "His children?" Tsardines.

23. Did you hear about John? He bought a Louis XIV bed but it was too small for him so he sent it back and ordered a Louis XV.

24. They have a telephone dial system for atheists. You dial a number and no one answers.

25. "Why did you get drunk in the first place?" "I didn't get drunk in the first place. I got drunk in the last place."

26. I was watching a TV movie and they had a bad man who was so mean, ornery and quick-on-the-draw that they had to call in the Marshals from three other channels to whip him.

27. Dentist to talkative patient: "Open your mouth and shut up."

28. A patient with a sore foot came to see the Doctor. The nurse ordered him to take off all his clothes. He complained to the man in the next cubicle who had also been ordered to strip. That man complained: "I only came in to fix the phone."

29. A government bureau is where the taxpayer's shirt is kept.

30. A diplomat is a man who knows how far he can go before he has gone too far.

31. A Minister was conducting the funeral of a Deacon. In his eulogy, he pointed to the corpse and declared that the soul had left. "What you see here is just the shell, the nut has departed."

32. "I'll accept your opinion for what it's worth. You owe me ten dollars."

33. A very self-important dowager: "My ancestors did not come over on the Mayflower; they had their own boat!"

34. "I give in, lady. What's the use? It's my word against thousands of yours."

35. "I like you better the more I see you less!"

36. One supervisor to another while watching the employees stream out at closing time: "Am I losing my hearing or are they faster than sound?"

37. The Prime Minister of Israel, in declining a Burmese gift of an elephant, said that his rule was never to accept a gift that eats.

38. A Norwegian ice factory was forced to close when they lost the recipe.

39. A sign observed in a factory: "Firings will continue until morale improves."

40. The most famous Norwegian inventor was Henry Fjord.

41. A Swedish race car driver entered the Indianapolis 500. He had to make 75 pit stops; 3 for gas and tires and 72 to get directions.

42. If I'd known you were coming, I'd have faked an ache.

43. An Ohio woman complained to police that a thief not only stole milk from her doorstep but had left orders for whipping cream.

44. A political war is where everybody shoots from the lip.

45. A diplomat is one who thinks twice before he says nothing.

46. Harry Truman was Nancy Reagan's favorite piano player. Just the other night I thought she had on one of his records. It turned out to be a spoon that was caught in the garbage disposal.

47. "Our guest of honor tonight is a humble and a modest man—and with good reason."

48. We play "Hail to the Chief" when the President makes an entrance. Congress should have its own song too when it convenes: "Send in the Clowns."

49. W.C. Fields: "They had a butler who drank too much—sort of an old family container."

50. Sign at a bar: "Lunch now being poured."

51. Hell hath no fury like the lawyer of a woman scorned.

52. "How do you feel?" asked a nurse as she was drawing blood from a donor. He said: "I feel like I want to go home."

53. An actor said that his memory was perfect now, ever since he took the Sam Carnegie course.

54. I was taking a course to improve my memory but I forgot where the school is.

55. Asked the young woman: "Do you think thirty years is too great a difference in age between a man and a woman where he's the President of a bank?"

56. I was going to read the report about the rising crime rate—but somebody stole it.

57. Obesity in this country is widespread.

58. Anything with a handle means work.

59. "Where did you learn to sing?" "I took a correspondence course." "You must have lost a lot of your mail."

60. A lawyer stayed up all night trying to break a widow's Will.

61. Sign on a Washington Pentagon desk: "The secrecy of my job does not permit me to know what I am doing."

62. The inhabitants of Paris are called Parasites.

63. Exasperated mother to child at dinner: "Eat it, darling, pretend it's mud."

64. It was so windy the other day that a chicken laid the same egg four times.

65. Definition of frustration: Buying a new boomerang and finding it impossible to throw the old one away.

66. An Australian inventor was the first to combine a boomerang and a hand grenade. He was also the last.

67. Every man needs a wife because too many things go wrong that can't be blamed on the government.

68. A certain town was so quiet that they had to cancel the curfew because it woke people up.

69. It's an ill wind that blows a saxophone.

70. He's as careful as a nudist climbing over a barbed wire fence.

71. The ten best years of a woman's life are between 28 and 30.

72. An egotist is writing a book: "Famous people who have known me."

73. How to save on defense: Use last year's rockets but add new grills.

74. A man lived in an apartment where the walls were so thin that when he hung a picture, he had his next door neighbor bend over the nails.

75. If I have twelve oranges and I give you three, how many do I have left? Student: "I don't know. In our school, we only studied apples."

76. Bridegroom, at the altar: "I thee endow with all of my worldly goods." His father: "There goes his bicycle."

77. Knowledge is power if you know it about the right people.

78. In our society, a man is known by the company he owns.

79. Diplomat: a man who convinces his wife that she looks stout in a mink coat.

80. A kibitzer is a guy with an interferiority complex.

81. Teacher: "What is the best way to keep milk from souring?" Student: "Leave it in the cow."

82. Did you have any trouble with your French while you were in Paris? No, but the French people did.

83. Mothers-in-law are a lot like seeds: they come with the tomato.

84. A billing clerk consulted a psychiatrist: he kept hearing strange invoices.

85. I know a woman who had sixteen children. She got a divorce on the grounds of compatibility.

86. Life has been described as a tree, the tree of life. And man is the sap running through it.

87. They have just invented plastic song sheets for people who sing in the shower.

88. At the intersections of some of the big cities, they have teleprompters that say: "Walk." "Don't Walk." "Run like hell."

89. A man bought an expensive hearing aid costing $2,500. He was asked what kind it was. He responded: "A quarter to five."

90. A divorce was based on religious grounds: The wife worshipped money and the husband didn't have any.

91. A traveler returning to the United States from abroad was challenged by a customs agent as to whether he had any pornographic material. He replied: "I don't even have a pornograph."

92. Is that all there is to the story? Yes, I've already told you more than I heard.

93. A man who was employed to stamp grapes in a wine factory was fired because he kept sitting down on the job.

94. Picasso was struck by a hit-and-run driver. He was asked to draw a sketch of the driver. The next day the police arrested three suspects: a nun, the Eiffel tower and a TV set.

95. The government is like a huge elephant that sits on a baby bird to keep it warm.

96. I'm neither for nor against apathy.

97. During the New Hampshire primaries, a baby had been kissed by so many candidates that she developed chapped cheeks.

98. I hate intolerant people.

99. Newspaper advertisement: "Earn cash in your spare time—blackmail your friends."

100. Secretary to boss: "I've got good news and bad news." Boss: "Give me the good news first." Secretary: "You're not sterile."

101. Owensburg, Kentucky, *News:* The baseball game continued in the cow pasture and ended when a runner slid into what he thought was third base.

102. Pasadena, California, *Independent:* Mrs. Williams was acclaimed champion rolling pin thrower; her husband won the 100 yard dash and the chicken race.

103. Candidate: I would swallow my pride but I hate junk food.

104. Joggers and jogging are not to be sniffed at.

105. They've developed a new U.S. embassy building for use in unfriendly countries that comes with the windows already broken.

106. The only time I've seen a flying saucer was once when a nudist spilled hot coffee on his lap.

107. Speaker: "I have a few examples but I haven't decided yet what they illustrate."

108. A natural skier is one whose bones knit fast.

109. Senator, on a hunting expedition: "Let's miss two more rabbits and then call it a day."

110. A man visiting a nudist colony reported that the butler (completely nude) answered the door. Question: If he was nude, how did you know it was the butler? Answer, after careful consideration: "Well, it certainly wasn't the maid."

111. Problem today: How to tell whether a woman's clothes have shrunk.

112. A man saw a sign reading: "Drink Canada Dry"—and he's been up there trying ever since.

113. A Scotsman had a stroke while playing golf and his companions made him count it.

114. A man lived in an apartment that was so small that when he stuck the key in the door he broke the window.

115. Why do the Scottish bagpipe players always march when they play? Answer: Because it's harder to hit a moving target.

116. A juror in New York asked to be excused because he said he could only hear out of one ear. The judge refused to excuse him, saying: "In this Court we hear only one side at a time."

117. A business man said he never reads mail addressed: "From the desk of..." because he doesn't believe in corresponding with furniture.

118. A small boy said that when he grew up, he wanted to be a fanatic.

119. If a bird flies into a fan, you get shredded tweet.

120. A Sunday golfer said it was a toss-up whether he would go to church or play golf. He said he had to toss up 15 times.

121. It's difficult to teach a new dog old tricks.

122. A Polish pharmacist was fired after he told his boss that he couldn't get the bottles into the typewriter.

123. A teacher instructed the parent to get an encyclopedia for his son. The parent responded: "Nothing doing. He can walk to school like I did."

124. A young man who was engaged to four girls at the same time explained that Cupid must have shot him with a machine gun.

125. Scoreboard at a Roman coliseum: Lions 21, Christians 6.

126. A farmer who was running a steam roller over his field explained that he was going to raise mashed potatoes.

127. Success expert: "What's your name?" Greek client: "POPAPOLOUS." Success expert: "You should get a job selling motorcycles."

128. If something can't go on forever, it will end.

129. A sign at a large corporation headquarters: "If you're not here on Saturday, don't bother to show up on Sunday."

130. A man comes to a psychiatrist with a cabbage hanging from one ear, a string of carrots around his neck and a bracelet of olives, and says: "I came here to see you about my brother."

131. Incentive plan for a company (sign): "One mistake and you're fired."

132. I can't swim much but I can wade like hell.

133. What's your name? T'T'T'T'T'T'Tom. I'll just call you Tom for short.

SOAP

134. It's reported that Jimmy Baker and Jimmy Swaggert are starting a new magazine: "Repent House."

135. Mark Russell says that the Mayor of Washington, DC has swept so much under the rug that he must walk uphill to get behind his desk.

136. "Doctor, will I be able to play the piano after the operation?" Doctor: "Yes, I am sure you can." Patient: "That's great, Doctor. I never could before."

137. Do you exercise after the morning bath? Yes, I generally step on the soap as I get out of the tub.

138. She skated hours on end.

139. Sign outside theater: "Seats are $4.50, $5.00 and $5.50. Standing room prices according to shoe size."

140. Judge: "Order. Order in the Court." Prisoner: "Make mine ham and cheese on rye, please."

141. Patient to psychiatrist: "I feel schizophrenic." Doctor: "That makes four of us."

142. Phyllis Diller willed her body to science but science is contesting the Will.

143. Elizabeth Taylor is building a halfway house for girls who don't want to go all the way.

144. Dean Martin is considering filling his swimming pool with martinis. He claims that that will make it impossible to drown since the deeper you sink, the higher you'll get.

145. Robert Benchley said, after coming in out of the rain: "I must get out of these wet clothes and into a dry martini."

146. Patient: "My ear rings all the time; what can I do, Doctor?" Doctor: "Get an unlisted ear."

147. My father used to talk to me. He'd say: "Listen, stupid." He always called me "listen."
Henny Youngman.

148. A stock market investor is someone who is alert, informed, attuned to the economic heartbeat of America—and cries a lot.

149. A mummy is an Egyptian who has been pressed for time.

150. They've invented a new kind of Indian roulette. You sit beside a snake charmer with six cobras; one of them is deaf.

151. Mrs. Upton's dog has been run over. She will be heart broken. Don't tell her abruptly. "No, I'll begin by saying it's her husband."

152. Personally, I felt a lot more secure in 1933 when all I had to fear was fear itself.

153. To forgive is divine. It helps clear the moral traffic jams. They should have an express lane for people with six sins or less.

154. A jury is a group of twelve people of average ignorance.

155. If you don't go away and leave me alone, I'll find someone who will.

156. Adlai Stevenson: A politician is a person who approaches every subject with an open mouth.

157. "I hate my mother-in-law," said one cannibal to another at dinner. Responded the other: "Then, just eat your vegetables."

158. "And there, son, you have the story of your dad during World War II." "Yes, Dad, but why did they need all the other soldiers?"

159. Drunk to bar tender: "Hey, gimme a horse's neck." Second drunk: "I'll have a horse's tail; there's no sense killing two horses."

160. A father fed his baby garlic so he could find him in the dark.

161. In Russia recently, burglars broke into the Secret Police Headquarters and stole next year's election returns.

162. There are more important things in life than money. The trouble is that they all cost money.

163. They had a rough day at the office. The computer broke down and everyone had to learn to think all over again.

164. Tourist circular: In backward countries, don't drink the water and in the progressive societies, don't breathe the air.

165. John Wayne played a dual role in the movie: General Sherman and the entire Union Army.

166. Why did they hang that picture? Answer: "They could not find the artist."

167. Missionary: "Why are you looking at me so intently?" Cannibal: "I'm the food inspector."

168. "Is that a popular song he is singing?" "It was before he sang it."

169. Sheriff: "Did you catch the auto thief?" Deputy: "He was a lucky bird; we had chased him only about a mile when our 500 miles was up and we had to stop and change the oil."

170. "What became of the big man who used to beat the base drum?" He quit; he got so fat that when he marched, he couldn't hit the drum in the middle.

171. I just took a bath in the market. I bought 300 shares of Consolidated Union Suit, then the bottom fell out.

172. A sad story: a confused little kid who was running around a harem trying to celebrate Mother's Day.

173. I read about one of the most expensive movies ever made. It cost two million dollars just for the intermission.

174. My dad believed in meditation—he used to tell me to sit down and shut up.

175. You think you've got troubles. I know a fellow who's been going to a psychiatrist for five years. He just found out the guy's deaf.

176. Definition of a minute man: a guy who can make it to the refrigerator, fix a sandwich and a short beer, and be back before the commercial is over.

177. "Are you a college man?" "No, a horse just stepped on my hat."

178. Minister: "You must pay for your sins. If you have already paid, you can ignore this notice."

179. A letter to Ann Landers asked what it meant that a lady's husband went hunting but forgot his gun. Her answer: "He doesn't intend to shoot what he's going to hunt."

180. A woman bought a large economy size can of aerosol hair spray, took it home, pressed the aerator button—and blew off her arm.

181. A boy got into a fight with one of two identical twins next door and gave him a black eye, explaining that he did so so that he could tell them apart.

182. A manufacturer said his business was running 50-50; an order in the morning and a cancellation in the afternoon.

183. A county in Arizona is named "Cactus Junction." They have so much cactus in the county that they have to keep moving the county seat.

184. I have a friend who drowned while taking acupuncture on a waterbed.

185. A priest in Chicago was asked if he wasn't worried when he carried the gold cross. He replied: "Not if I carry it fast enough."

186. Don't worry about flying. It's not dangerous. Crashing is dangerous.

187. Have you heard about the tree surgeon who fell out of his patient?

188. The less you have to do with him, the less you'll be worse off.

189. *Pittsburgh Press:* "I work for the Pittsburgh Natural Gas Company. Over 90% of the people in Pittsburgh have gas."

190. *San Francisco Bulletin:* "Eleven of the twenty children were boys. Fourteen are living and seven married."

191. Mountain View (CA) *Pictorial News:* "Men's Activity Night starts March 25 in the girl's gym."

192. *Boston Globe:* "The font so generously given by Mrs. Smith will be set in position in the East end of the church. Now, babies may be baptized at both ends."

193. Denver *Rocky Mountain News:* "His first venture into the antique field was in Asheville, NC. There, he met his wife."

194. "Did you take a bath today?" "Why, is one missing?"

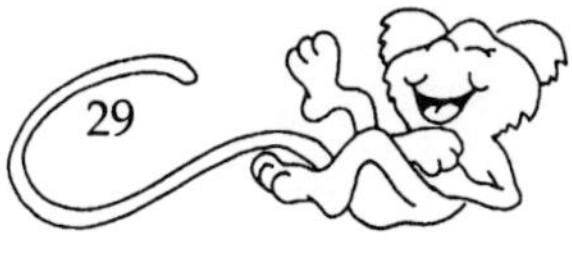

195. "How do you make anti freeze?" "Steal her blanket."

196. A lady had so many face lifts that every time she raises her eyebrows, she pulls up her stockings.

197. Count to Three. See if you can do it from memory.

198. Waiter: "How was the soup?" "To tell you the truth, I'm really sorry I stirred it."

199. "I never forget a face but in your case I'm willing to make an exception."

200. In Iowa, they have three grades of gas— regular, premium and whole wheat.

201. If women want to wear those real short shorts, I'm behind them all the way.

202. People in Hollywood get married so many times. I went to a PTA meeting where there were 400 parents for sixteen kids.

203. A Mormon had too many wives. The IRS told him that he must tell all but one of the wives that they must go. He replied: "No, you tell them."

204. One Senator: "Senator James is his own worst enemy." The other Senator: "Not while I'm alive."

205. An Indian baby is called a caboose.

206. A man who has more than one wife is called a pigamist.

207. A fanatic is a person who can't change his mind and won't change the subject.

208. Marine Sergeant: "Men, I have good news and bad news. The good news: You get to change underwear. The bad news: You have to change with each other. Ted with Bill, etc."

209. If all the people who sleep in church were laid end to end, they would be much more comfortable.

210. Art Carney complained to Jackie Gleason that he had a mental block. Jackie responded: "I think your mental block is made of cement."

211. An ugly American hero won the French Croix de Guerre but they couldn't find a French General who, in presenting the medal, was willing to kiss him.

212. A closed mouth gathers no foot.

213. Two movie stars passed each other at the door to the psychiatrist's office. One asked: "Are you coming or going?" The other: "If I knew that, I wouldn't be here."

214. A minister, who told his congregation that he had identified 739 separate sins, said that he had already received 73 requests for the list.

215. A sharp nose indicates curiosity. A flattened nose indicates too much curiosity.

216. A barking dog never bites—while barking.

217. You know the old proverb: A barking dog never bites. Yes, you know the proverb and I know the proverb but the question is, does the dog know the proverb?

218. Wife: "Before our marriage you said you were well off." Husband: "I was, but I didn't realize it."

219. A man was fired from his job with the Sanitation Department because he couldn't keep his mind in the gutter.

220. Lawyer: "Tell the Court why you stabbed your husband 58 times." Wife: "I didn't know how to turn off the electric knife."

221. I didn't know your wife could do the Charleston. Husband: "She isn't doing it; the waiter spilled some hot soup down her back."

222. One doctor to another: "I take two aspirin every four patients."

223. Siberian dogs are the fastest in the world because the trees are so far apart.

224. I never remember a name but I always forget a face.

225. Lady to a sales clerk: "Please show me a dress to match my eyes." Clerk: "I'm sorry madam, but we don't have any bloodshot dresses."

226. I'm reading an unusual murder mystery. It seems the victim was shot by a man from another book.

227. A Kangaroo complained to his psychiatrist: "I don't know what's the matter with me. I just don't feel jumpy any more."

228. They've invented a new toothpaste with the food particles built right in for people who can't eat before brushing.

229. Sign in a restaurant; "Our tongue sandwiches speak for themselves."

230. Politician: "I sleep like a baby. I go to sleep for an hour, then wake up crying."

231. Archie Bunker: "Certainly, I'm innocent, Edith, but of what?"

232. Archie Bunker: "Was uncle's death untimely, you ask? Well, it was near lunch."

233. Kissinger: "The rest of the story is how I saved the world."

234. Judge to an applicant for citizenship: "Do you solemnly swear to support the Constitution?" Applicant: "Judge, I'd like to but I have a wife and eight children in Europe."

235. Lawyer to Judge: "Judge, my client stole the ring in a moment of weakness." Judge: "I suppose if he had had a moment of strength, he would have stolen the safe."

236. A Texas merchant asked the police to help him decipher the signature on a worthless check. The police did. It read: "U. R. Stuck."

237. A Lewiston, Maine, judge refused to send a thief to the County jail because, the last time, he had kicked about the food too much.

238. A woman in Texas won a divorce after telling the judge that whenever she started to tell her side of an argument, her husband shut off his hearing aid.

239. A West Virginia landscaper was supervising a group working to sod a new lawn. He had to keep shouting: "Green side up."

240. An Irishman moved his house back fifty feet to take up the slack in his clothes line.

241. Recently, we heard of an Iraqi bookkeeper who absconded with the accounts payable.

242. A magician said that his best trick was sawing a woman in half. When asked if he had any brothers or sisters, he replied that he had six half sisters.

243. A nurse was asked why she had a rectal thermometer behind her ear. "My goodness," she exclaimed, "now I remember where I put my ball point pen."

244. Headline in the *Minneapolis Star*: "April babies flood local hospital."

245. If you cross the Frankenstein monster with a hot dog, you get a Frankenfurterstein.

246. "Where's your brother"? Answer: "He's in the house playing a duet. I finished first."

247. A doctor ordered a patient to have not more than one drink a day. The patient reported that he was following orders and was up to March 5, 1995. (This was March, 1989.)

248. The Norwegian government has been having trouble with its space program. Their astronaut keeps falling off the kite.

249. A man got a crazy new diet of nothing but powdered food, then got caught in a rainstorm and gained twenty pounds.

250. "Please stand in front of my car and tell me if the blinker is working." "Yes" "No" "Yes" "No" "Yes" "No" "Yes"

251. Supervisor to employee: "Did you call John (a fellow employee) a liar?" "Yes." "Stupid?" "Yes." "A slave driver?" "Yes." "An opinionated bull headed egomaniac?" "No, but would you write that down so I can remember it?"

252. What this country needs is a man who can be right and President at the same time.

253. "Doctor, how soon will I know anything when I come out of the anesthetic?" Doctor: "Well, that's expecting a lot out of an anesthetic."

254. Now and then a collision occurs when two motorists go after the same pedestrian.

255. A dachshund is half a dog high and a dog and a half long. It is bought by parents who want to make it possible for all the children to pet it at the same time.

256. What do you find the most difficult thing on the piano? "Paying the installments."

257. A farmer named his rooster Robinson because he crew so.

258. Illegal foreigners are swarming into the U.S.—it's about out of control. Proposal: to put the man who found the two contaminated grapes (and thereby destroyed a billion dollars worth of Chilean fruit) in charge of immigration.

259. A man convicted of killing his third wife was asked why he cracked her skull; he explained that his first two wives died of eating poisoned mushrooms but his third wife refused them.

260. Some men went fishing through the ice in Blackduck, Minnesota. They had bad luck, explaining that by the time they chopped a hole big enough for the boat, they were all worn out.

261. L.B. Mayer. "In life, you must learn to take the bitter with the sour."

262. Warren Buffet, on the average holding period for stocks in his Mutual Fund: "Our average holding period is forever."

263. Student: "Why does the whistle blow for a fire?" His friend: "It doesn't blow for the fire, it blows for the water. They've already got the fire."

264. If a lad has a stepfather, is the boy a stepladder?

265. A boy told his father that he was kept in after school because he did not know where the Azores were. Father: "Well, in the future, just remember where you put things."

266. Before we begin the test, are there any questions? Student: "What is the name of this course?"

267. Telephone: "Is Hugh there?" "Hugh who?" "Hugh hoo yourself."

268. "Allow me to present my wife to you." "Many thanks, but I already have one."

269. Why do you play golf so much? It keeps me fit. What for? Golf.

270. Sign on Scottish golf course: "Members will refrain from picking up lost balls until they have stopped rolling."

271. Politicians are like rocking chairs. They're only level when you're sitting on them.

272. A miser was mad, in leaving the hospital, because he got well before his pills were gone.

273. Movie tough: "Shoot low, boys, they're riding Shetland ponies." Lewis Grizzard.

274. Henny Youngman: If I'm not in bed by 11 P.M., I go home.

275. "Cast your bread upon the waters and you'll get back ten soggy loaves."

276. When I was born, my parents ran away from home.

277. In Russia, a pessimist is one who thinks things can't get any worse. An optimist thinks they can.

278. A prostate operation is now called a low botomy.

279. Calvin Coolidge: "When more and more people are thrown out of work, unemployment results."

280. "I've had many cases of love that were just infatuation, but this hatred I feel for you is the real thing."

281. Burglar to his wife who was nagging him for money: "Okay, Okay, I'll get you some just as soon as the bank closes."

282. A secret: something you tell to only one person at a time.

283. Our stone age ancestors deserve more credit. Think of the cunning and strength it took to hunt dinosaurs. The decoy alone weighed three tons.

284. Mexican radio announcer: "At the sound of the tone, the time will be exactly 9 o'clock—or maybe 9:15."

285. Small boy: "In the old days, did the knights fight with battle axes?" Father: "Well, the married ones did."

286. Speaker: "In all sincerity, I want to say that of all the introductions that I have ever had, that that — (pause) — was the most recent."

287. W.C. Fields: "After two days in the hospital, I took a turn for the nurse."

288. Chinese proverb: Many men smoke but foo men choo.

289. Do you file your fingernails? No, I just throw them away.

290. Psychiatrist: "I wouldn't worry about your son making mud pies. It's quite normal." Mother: "I don't think so and neither does his wife."

291. The hardest thing to learn is which bridge to burn and which to cross.

292. Would you like your mother-in-law embalmed? Cremated? Buried? "That'll be fine."

293. The trouble with opera is that there's too much singing.

294. Opera is Italian vaudeville where you get stabbed and, instead of bleeding, you sing.

295. One psychiatrist advertises: "A cure guaranteed or your mania back."

296. He has such a big mouth that he can eat a banana—sideways.

297. Success hasn't changed him—he's still the same arrogant bum he always was.

298. He hasn't an enemy in the world but all his friends hate him.

299. My wife insisted on picking my new secretary—and he's a nice fellow too.

300. Two English ladies are talking at tea. First lady: "Breeding is everything, isn't it?" Other lady: "No, but it's lots of fun."

301. The miracle drugs are marvelous. Now, a doctor can keep a patient alive until he pays his bill.

302. If it wasn't for half of the people in the world, the other half would be all of them.

303. Member of hunting party to guide: " I thought you said you were the best guide in Vermont." Guide: " I did, but I think we're in Canada."

304. Practical nurse: one who marries a rich patient.

305. I go to the opera whether I need the sleep or not.

306. W.C. Fields: "Once during the prohibition, I was forced for days to live on nothing but food and water."

307. One out of four people in this country is mentally unbalanced. Think of your three closest friends. If they seem OK, you're the one.

308. Sign on back of truck in New York: "Help keep New York clean; dump your garbage in New Jersey.

309. Doctor, I demand a second opinion. "Okay, I'll tell you again."

310. *Nolo contendere* is a legal term meaning: "Not guilty and I won't do it again."

311. "Old age" is when you sit in a rocking chair and you can't get it going.

312. A TV network is planning a 2-hour special. A Norwegian will attempt to count to 100.

313. A great medical breakthrough: The East Germans have performed the first successful hernia transplant.

314. Rural life is found mostly in the country.

315. Newspaper headline: "County officials talk rubbish."

316. The circus manager refused to let the human cannon ball quit, asking: "Where can I find another man of your calibre?"

317. Everything comes to him who orders hash.

318. You take him with you when you want to be alone.

319. He's not a bad guy until you get to know him.

320. A communist is one who borrows your pot to cook your goose in.

321. Our national flower is the concrete cloverleaf.

322. We had a letter yesterday from the undertaker. He said that if the last installment isn't paid on your grandmother within seven days, "up she comes."

323. Two can live as cheaply as one for half as long.

324. Any time a person feels lonely and neglected, he should think of Whistler's father.

325. At the airport, a man went up to the counter and said: "I'll take two chances on your flight to Miami."

326. Barber, to customer: "Haven't I shaved you before?" Customer: "No, I got that scar in the war."

327. A man has invented a sprinkling can without any holes in the spout for people who have artificial flowers.

328. Lilly Tomlin: "We're all in this alone."

329. Psychiatrist to Saddam Hussein: "No, you're not paranoid. The whole world really is out to get you."

330. In a cooperative dancing school, they've even got concave instructors for the very fat students.

331. Defeat isn't bitter if you don't swallow it.

332. If your wife wants to learn to drive, don't stand in her way.

333. Now that prayer is forbidden in schools, you have to go to a motel to read the Bible.

334. You can't make footprints in the sands of time sitting down.

335. Why did you put sand in Richard's mouth? "It was open."

336. How did Billy break your hammer? "I hit him over the head with it."

337. A Psychiatrist has discovered a new kind of shock treatment: he sends the bill in advance.

338. If you die in an elevator, be sure to push the UP button.

339. Mark Twain: "He had no principles and was delightful company."

340. Today is the tomorrow you worried about yesterday.

341. There are three things I can't remember: "Names, faces—and I can't remember what the third thing is."

342. She took him for better or worse, but he was worse than she took him for.

343. The famous trial lawyer, Clarence Darrow: "Calvin Coolidge was the greatest man ever to come out of Plymouth Corner, Vermont."

344. Will Rogers: "Oklahomans will vote dry as long as any citizen can stagger to the polls."

345. Definition of a farmer: "A man who is outstanding in his field."

346. An ad in a Pittsburgh paper: "For sale. Second hand tombstone. Excellent buy for someone named Murphy."

347. "Are you the barber who cut my hair the last time?" "No sir, I've only worked here a year."

348. "Doctor, Doctor!" screamed the young mother, "my son just swallowed a 45 calibre bullet." Doctor: "Okay, lady. Give him two tablespoons of castor oil before putting him to bed. In the meantime, don't point him at anyone."

349. Doctor: "Open wide. Wider. Your throat is OK but you're going to have trouble with your stomach. You swallowed my stick."

350. A mother explained to the camp counselor that her son was very sensitive and high strung, and that if her son behaved badly at any time, she asked that the counselor hit the boy next to him. That would startle him into behaving.

351. The average man's idea of a good sermon is one that goes over his head and hits one of his neighbors.

352. Try praising your wife even if it does frighten her at first.

353. Josh Billings: One of the best temporary cures for pride and snobbishness is seasickness; a man who wants to vomit never puts on airs.

354. A specialist is a doctor whose patients can only be ill during regular office hours.

355. A pessimist is one who feels bad when he feels good for fear he'll feel worse when he feels better.

356. A man in a washroom found this message posted over one of those hot air blowers for drying hands: "Push button for a short message from the Vice President."

357. Bumper sticker: "Whoever has the most things when he dies, wins."

358. Sign on Chinese laundry: "We don't tear your clothes with clumsy machinery. We do it carefully by hand."

359. A toastmaster is a guy who goes around introducing people who need no introduction.

360. Dignity is window dressing for an empty store.

361. Early to bed and early to rise, and you'll meet very few of our best people.

362. Henny Youngman: "Some people ask the secret of our long marriage. We take time to go to a restaurant two times a week—a little candle light, dinner, soft music and dancing: She goes Tuesdays and I go Fridays."

363. An army sergeant is driving around with special license plates: HUP 234.

364. The two great disappointments of life: Not getting what you want, and getting it.

365. Washington is the only city where sound travels faster than light.

366. President Reagan: "I do not dye my hair. It's just prematurely orange."

367. Sign on car: Sex Appeal—Give Generously.

368. Woody Allen: "My wife was very immature. I'd be in the bathroom taking a bath and she'd walk right in and sink my boats."

369. He died at twenty but was buried at seventy.

370. I don't know what I'd do without you but I'm willing to try.

371. Doesn't that mule ever kick you? No, but he frequently kicks de place where I recently was.

372. Never miss an opportunity to make others happy even if you have to leave them alone to do it.

373. A guide explained that the huge rock formations were piled up there by the glaciers. A curious old lady: "But where are the glaciers now?" Guide: "They've gone back to get more rocks."

374. Cynic: "At the end of the evening my wife was so tired that she could hardly keep her mouth open."

375. A man was so far down on his luck that he didn't dare scratch matches on the bottom of his shoes because it tore his socks.

376. Mae West fainted and it took four men to carry her out, going two abreast.

377. Husband complained to wife that she spent four hours at the beauty parlor. Her reply: "That was just for the estimate."

378. P.T. Barnum advertised a man-eating chicken, and that's what it turned out to be: a man eating chicken.

379. A fireworks factory in South Dakota blew up with such an explosion that the city in now located in North Dakota.

380. A football player was so rich that he had an unlisted number on his jersey.

381. A boy was glad he wasn't born in Russia because he didn't know how to speak Russian.

382. Ad in a New York paper: "Piano moving; expert handling. Careful moving a must with us. Also, kindling wood for sale."

No 1

383. A cannibal mother and her child saw an airplane fly over. Child to mother: "What's that?" Mother: "It's something like a lobster; you only eat what's inside."

384. A man calls the fire department and shouts: "Hurry! Hurry! Come put out the fire in my house." Fireman: "How do we get to your house?" The anxious man: "Don't you still have that big red truck any more?"

385. They've invented a dry canal for barges with wheels.

386. In Miami, a man was held up so many times that he developed tan armpits.

387. An Indianapolis publisher received an unsolicited manuscript titled: "How to Make Your Own Mink Coat." The opening line: "First, catch 62 mink."

388. An army sergeant asked if he could take a tank home because he was teaching his wife how to drive.

389. Sign on a plumber's window: "Do it yourself. Then call us before it's too late."

390. The musical "Oklahoma" was performed in Russia but they had to change the words: "Oh, what a beautiful tractor; Oh, what a lovely machine. Maybe I shouldn't have backed it into the tomb of Lenin."

391. Last week the boss doubled my salary. I used to get $150 every week. Now I get $150 every two weeks.

392. A Dad told his son that once, when he went out for track, he jumped twelve feet—that was when he accidentally backed into a javelin.

393. Around 1700, because of all the dissatisfactions in England, the two political parties—the Whigs and Tories—came into being so that people could be more specific about what it was they hated.

394. Congressman: "Gentlemen, I wish to tax your memory." Other Congressman: "Why didn't I think of that?"

395. Customer to waitress: "What is this fly doing in my soup?" Waitress, after close studied observation: "I don't know but I think it's the side stroke."

396. My problem is that it takes me 6 weeks to read the book of the month.

397. Newspaper headline: "Gene Autry is better after being kicked by a horse."

398. Ziggy complained to his veterinarian that something was wrong with his goldfish. He seemed to lack a goal in life.

399. The wedding was an eight-Kleenex affair.

400. Napoleon: "Religion is what keeps the poor people from murdering the rich."

401. Money is always there, but the pockets change.

402. J. Paul Getty: "The meek shall inherit the earth—but not the mineral rights.

403. If you think education is expensive, try ignorance.

404. My grandmother is over eighty and still doesn't need glasses. Drinks right out of the bottle. Henny Youngman.

405. Victor Borge: "I know only two pieces. One is Clair de Lune, and the other one isn't.

406. Message on fortune cookie: "Ignore previous cookie."

407. Only dead fish swim with the stream.

408. Marriage is the only war where you sleep with the enemy.

409. Millions long for immortality who don't know what to do on a rainy Sunday afternoon. Susan Erzt.

410. Veni Vidi Visa. "I came. I saw. I went shopping."

411. Phyllis Diller: "I was in a beauty contest once. I not only came in last. I was hit in the mouth by Miss Congeniality."

412. "I used to work in a fire hydrant factory. You couldn't park anywhere near the place." Steven Wright.

413. W.C. Fields: "Start every day with a smile and get it over with."

414. Never keep up with the Joneses. Drag them down to your level. Quenton Crisp.

415. I shot an arrow into the air and it stuck. Graffito.

416. Fred Allen: He was the world's only armless sculptor. He put the chisel in his mouth and his wife hit him on the back of the head with a mallet.

417. Psychiatry is the care of the id by the odd.

418. The more he talked of his honor, the faster we counted our spoons. Ralph Waldo Emerson.

419. The future is much like the present, only longer. Don Quisenberry.

420. I keep a rock garden; last week, three of them died. R. Duran.

421. "Is this the party to whom I am speaking?" Lily Tomlin.

422. "Happiness is good health and a bad memory." Ingrid Bergman.

423. "We must believe in luck; for how else can we explain the success of those we don't like." Jean Cocteau.

424. "I just got wonderful news from my Florida real estate agent. They found land on my property." Milton Berle.

425. I'm in favor of liberalized immigration because of the effect it would have on the restaurants. I'd let in just about everybody except the English.

426. The most remarkable thing I remember about my mother is that for thirty years she served the family with nothing but leftovers. The original meal has never been found. Calvin Trillin.

427. "When My Love Comes Back From the Ladies' Room Will I Be Too Old To Care." Title of Lewis Grizzard song.

428. Lewis Grizzard book title: "They Tore Out My Heart and Stamped the Sucker Flat."

429. Schizophrenia beats eating alone.

430. The less things change, the more they stay the same.

431. "Never go to a doctor whose office plants have died." Erma Bombeck.

432. "If called by a panther, don't anther." Ogden Nash.

433. "A cucumber should be well-sliced, dressed with pepper and vinegar, and then thrown out." Samuel Johnson.

434. "If people don't want to come out to the ball park, nobody's going to stop them." Yogi Berra.

435. Faith is believing what you know ain't so. Mark Twain.

436. Book Title: "How to Raise Your IQ by Eating Gifted Children."

437. I base my fashion taste on what doesn't itch. Gilda Radner.

438. Artemus Ward: "I have already given two cousins to the War and I stand ready to sacrifice my wife's brother."

439. "Join the army, see the world, meet interesting people, and kill them."

440. Billy Nye: "There must be 500,000 rats in the U.S.; of course, I am only speaking from memory.

441. Honest criticism is hard to take, particularly from a relative, a friend, an acquaintance, or a stranger. F.P. Adams

442. Roses are red, violets are blue, I'm schizophrenic and so am I. Frank Crow.

443. "He writes so well he makes me feel like putting my quill back in the goose." Fred Allen.

444. "Shut up, he explained." Ring Lardner.

445. "Never accept a drink from a urologist." Erma Bombeck's father.

446. The late, late Jimmy Hoffa: "I may have my faults, but being wrong ain't one of them."

447. Tallulah Bankhead: "I'm as pure as the driven slush."

448. Sportscaster after seeing a baseball player fall twice in the first inning: "He washed his legs today and can't do a thing with them."

449. "What's on your mind, if you will allow the overstatement." Fred Allen.

450. "I didn't want to be rich, I just wanted enough to get the couch reupholstered." Kate Mostel.

451. Groucho Marx: "Go, and never darken my towels again."

452. "The curtain rises on a vast primitive wasteland, not unlike certain parts of New Jersey."
Woody Allen.

453. "A doctor can bury his mistakes but an architect can only advise his client to plant vines."
Frank Lloyd Wright.

454. "I wish people who have trouble communicating would just shut up." Tom Lehrer.

455. "The race may not be to the swift nor the victory to the strong, but that's the way to bet." Damon Runyon.

456. Chamberlain's law: "Everything tastes more or less like chicken."

457. McCabe's law: "Nobody has to do anything."

458. Mark Twain: "I was gratified to be able to answer promptly. I said I didn't know."

459. "Until you walk a mile in another man's moccasins, you can't imagine the smell." Robert Byrne.

460. He was picked to be an astronaut because he had such a great sense of direction.

461. Lincoln: "He can compress the most words into the smallest idea of any man I ever met."

462. A man who was half Italian and half Chinese was named Video Pong.

463. Happiness is seeing Lubbock, Texas in the rear view mirror.

464. "It was such a primitive country we didn't even see any joggers." Hamilton Cartoon caption.

465. Sex is nobody's business except the 3 people involved.

466. Johnny Carson: "Nancy Reagan fell down and broke her hair."

467. "Never eat more than you can lift." Miss Piggy.

468. Golda Meir: "Don't be humble; you're not that great."

469. Memorial service: a farewell party for someone who has already left.

470. Mark Twain: "I would rather go to bed with Lillian Russell than with Ulysses S. Grant in full military regalia."

471. "What this country needs is more unemployed politicians." Edward Langley.

472. Groucho Marx: "Either this man is dead or my watch has stopped."

473. Everyone should believe in something. I believe I'll have another drink. W.C. Fields.

474. When Jimmy Carter's daughter Amy was asked if she had any message for the children of America, she replied: "No."

475. There are two kinds of people: Those who don't know and those who don't know that they don't know.

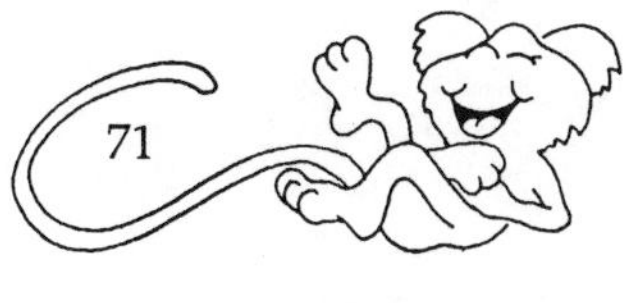

476. Cabbage: a vegetable about as large and wise as a man's head.

477. President Reagan: "I have left orders to be awakened at any time in case of national emergency, even if I'm in a cabinet meeting."

478. Most of our future lies ahead.

479. Charles Kraft: "Thanks to the Interstate Highway System it is now possible to travel from coast to coast without seeing anything."

480. President of United Airlines: "It is now possible for a flight attendant to get a pilot pregnant."

481. Winston Churchill: "History will be kind to me for I intend to write it."

482. Toast: "Here's to our wives and sweethearts; may they never meet." John Bunny.

483. Grand Forks, North Dakota, is not the end of the earth; but you can see it from there.

484. You can stand on a beer can in Fargo, North Dakota, and see the Montana border.

485. In North Dakota, snow doesn't melt. It wears itself out blowing back and forth.

486. One of the first things school children in Texas learn is how to compose a simple declarative sentence without the word SHIT in it.

487. FDR in a letter to Churchill: "It is fun being in the same decade with you."

488. Nixon: "It is the responsibility of the media to look at the President with a microscope, but they go too far when they use a proctoscope."

489. When he was elected Governor of California, Jack Warner said of Reagan; "It's our fault; we should have given him better parts."

490. W.C. Fields: "I never met a kid I liked."

491. Nobody ever bets enough on a winning horse.

492. "I've tried relaxing but—I don't know—I feel more comfortable, tense." Hamilton Cartoon caption.

493. A reformer is a guy who rides through a sewer in a glass bottomed boat.

494. A man is as young as the woman he feels.

495. If you want an audience, start a fight.
Gaelic proverb.

496. I don't like any of my loved ones.

497. W. Somerset Maugham: "I've always been interested in people but I've never liked them."

498. The empty taxi stopped and Jack Warner got out.

499. Jack Benny: "I don't deserve this award, but I have arthritis and I don't deserve that either."

500. Prince Charles sampled snake meat: "Boy, the things I do for England."

501. Mark Twain: Wagner's music isn't as bad as it sounds.

502. Jerry Reed song title: "She Got the Gold Mine; I Got the Shaft."

503. Kermit the frog: "It isn't easy being green."

504. Theodore Sturgem: "90% of everything is crap."

505. Truman: "I never did give anybody hell. I just told the truth and they thought it was hell."

506. Stay with me. I want to be alone. Joey Adams.

PHONE
PHONE
WALK
DON'T
WALK

507. The world is proof that God is a committee.
Bob Stokes.

508. Man in telephone booth at a busy intersection when describing his location over the phone, looked out the booth window and advised that he was at the corner of "Walk" and "Don't Walk."

509. If you put dirty things on paper, you can get sued unless you're a parakeet.

510. When I want your opinion, I'll give it to you.

511. Billy Martin was the only man in the world who could hear someone giving him the finger.

512. A man wanted to get a skunk out from under his house so he put some lutefisk there. The skunk left, but the problem then became how to get the Norwegian out from under it.

513. Pardon my bluntness but would you mind standing downwind.

514. A movie made 35 million—1 million on admissions and 34 million on the popcorn.

515. Husband: "What! Beans again? Wife: "I don't understand it. You liked beans on Monday, Tuesday, and Wednesday, and now—all of a sudden—you don't like beans.

516. A golfer reported that he never got mad when he played golf, and that he just laughed when he missed a shot. He said that when he played yesterday, he laughed 115 times.

517. Patient to doctor: "Doctor, how do I stand?" Doctor: "That's what puzzles me."

518. Sign in front of a Wisconsin dealership: "We stand behind all of our implements except the manure spreader."

519. A man, trying to lose weight, took up horseback riding. In the first week, the horse lost ten pounds.

520. A lady who went on a diet of bananas didn't lose any weight but you should see her climb trees!

521. When you mix holy water and prune juice, you get a religious movement.

522. A Midwestern man referred to his New York mother-in-law as the "wicked witch of the East."

523. Mother, to daughter: "If you don't want it, don't eat it. I'll put it in Daddy's lunch tomorrow."

524. The Swedes have bought 5 septic tanks. Just as soon as they learn how to drive them, they plan on invading Norway.

525. My take home pay won't take me home.

525. Firemen are reportedly always in heat.

526. Sign on truck: "Pass with care, I chew tobacco."

527. Sign: "Save water, bathe with a friend."

528. Sign on divorce lawyer's door: "Satisfaction guaranteed or your honey back."

529. Driver, nearing Chicago, saw a sign which read: "Chicago Left"; so he turned around and went back home.

530. A Chicago youth, in failing to report for army duty, said that the notice didn't state which year.

531. Wherever you go, there you are.

532. The Director of the Old Log Theater, on his newest highly successful play "Run for your Wife" said that "if you don't enjoy this play, we want you to come to the box office afterwards and we'll try to figure out what's wrong with you."

533. Sign in apartment building: "No baby carriages or foreign cars allowed in the lobby."

534. Young mother about her baby: "He's eating solids now—keys, pencils, bits of newspaper..."

535. Accountant to fellow employee: "That deficit had me worried for a minute; I forgot we were working for the government."

536. A man told his wife he wasn't drinking any more. He added *sotto voce* that he wasn't drinking any less either.

537. One bank is so big that it has a special window for holdups.

538. Two men discussing their new boss: "You can't help liking the guy; if you don't, he fires you."

Are you ready for more???

539. Sign seen on a local church: "Are Ye Weary Of Sin? Come In and Rest." Below it in pencil was written: "If not, call Baywater 11245."

540. Did the mudpack help your wife's appearance? It did for several days but then it fell off.

541. Man, to girlfriend: "Those lovely soft hands," he whispered, "that hair, and those beautiful eyes—where did you get those beautiful eyes?" "They came with the head," the girl replied.

542. My wife had an accident at the bank recently. She got in the wrong line and made a deposit.

543. They have a new drive-in bank that permits a husband to deposit from the front seat while his wife withdraws from the back seat.

544. Groucho Marx, in a letter: "I'm sorry your daughter Christie contemplates marrying a Swedish sailor; I didn't even know that they had a navy."

545. The child had every toy that his father ever wanted.

546. After the Civil War, Artemus Ward stopped in at a Southern eating place. He encountered a young man who accosted him thusly: "So, Sir, you come here to taunt us in our hour of trouble, do you?" "No" said he, "I come here for hash."

547. A farmer bought a farm a mile long and an inch wide. He plans to raise spaghetti.

548. The blood bank turned me down. They said they wanted plasma, not asthma.

549. When I went to the blood bank, they said they couldn't use me but would call me if they ever needed hot water.

550. "I celebrated my 23rd birthday yesterday." He: "What, again?"

551. Announcer: "At the sound of the gong, will someone please phone in the right time. Our clock stopped."

552. "Why did you hit your husband with a chair?" "I couldn't lift the table."

553. George Burns, to Playboy advisory staff: "I'd read your magazine more often, but my glasses keep steaming over."

554. My wife just got a mink coat. She gave it to herself for my birthday.

555. Groucho: "St. Paul, Minnesota, is only a stone's throw from Missouri; that is, if the stone is encased in a missile."

556. The United Nations keeps the peace. In forty years, there has never been a war in the UN building.

557. Burns: "Sam is in bed dying, with the family gathered around—and this wonderful aroma hits him. "Becky," he says, "isn't that chopped liver I smell?" "Yes, Sam, it is." He says: "Becky, one last time I gotta have some of that chopped liver." She says: "You can't; it's for after."

558. Song title: "I can't give you anything but love and a baby."

559. A man was saying grace in a low voice. Somebody at the table said: "I can't hear you." The man replied: "I wasn't talking to you."

560. Muhammed Ali: "My toughest fight was with my first wife."

561. For people who like peace and quiet, they've developed a phoneless cord.

562. My wife ran off with my best friend and I miss him, too.

563. Woody Allen was in a plane that was crashing. He said that a whole life flashed before him but it was the wrong life.

564. Yogi Berra was asked if he wanted his pizza in eight or twelve pieces. His answer: "You better make it eight, I don't think I could eat twelve pieces."

565. A man couldn't make it to a funeral, and asked a friend to go in his stead. The friend said he didn't know the deceased. The man said that was OK, that he should take the man's horse and the relatives would recognize the horse.

566. Letter to George Burns: "We're a young couple considering having a family. How far apart do you think children should be spaced?" Signed: "Anxious to get started."
"Dear Anxious, about five miles."

567. Burns: "If I have a problem, I don't take it to bed with me. I tell her to go home."

568. He sold me group insurance—but the whole group has to get sick before you collect.

569. Burns: "We were too poor to be fat. Our big Sunday dinner was bread and gravy. And you had to be careful not to get your fingers in the gravy or somebody would eat them."

570. Margaret Mead: "It's difficult to run an army if the General is in love with the Sergeant."

571. A man owns a bird that flies backwards. It's not interested in where it's going but in where it's been.

572. This being Easter Sunday, we will ask Mrs. B to come forward and lay an egg on the altar.

573. Senator Alan Simpson (R-WY), when asked his church preference, answers: "Red brick."

574. Professor: "This examination will be conducted on the honor system. Please take seats three seats apart and in alternate rows."

575. Is your husband a book worm? No, just an ordinary one.

576. Stout golfer's complaint: "When I put the ball where I can see it, I can't reach it and when I put it where I can reach it, I can't see it." (His reply when asked how he liked the game.)

577. District attorney to Plaintiff: "Are you sure this is the man who stole your car last Thursday?" Plaintiff: "Well, I was; but now, after the cross examination, I'm not sure I ever even owned a car."

578. A doctor was asked to prescribe a diet for a man who was reported to have HAGS disease (a combination of herpes, AIDS, gonorrhea and syphilis). When asked why he prescribed a diet of pancakes and pizza, he explained that those were the only things he could think of that could be slipped under the door.

579. A rooster crows early because he probably figures he can't get in a word edgewise after the hens get up.

580. One flaw in the jury system: It's a little frightening to have your fate in the hands of twelve people who weren't smart enough to get excused.

581. A stock market rally is where you have lost your shirt and you get back a sleeve.

582. Square meals make round people.

583. A goblet is a male turkey.

584. Thomas Edison told of the Boston man who was waiting for a total eclipse of the sun so that he could send a telegram at the special night rates.

585. Olaf Johnson wears dark glasses around the house, explaining that it bothers him to see his wife work so hard.

586. A man reported that he weighed 150 lbs. stooped over. He was asked: "Why stooped over?" His reply: "The scale is stuck under the kitchen sink."

587. "How is your wife's driving? Husband: "Last week she took a turn for the worse."

588. A speaker was criticized for approaching a vast subject with a half vast speech.

589. Ben Franklin: "To find out a girl's faults, praise her to her girlfriends."

590. A murderer is one who is presumed innocent until he is proven insane.

591. A psychiatrist had his office decorated with new furniture made of overwrought iron.

592. A bachelor is a man who prefers to cook his own goose.

593. Minister: "On the judgment day there will be weeping and the gnashing of teeth." One woman complained that she didn't have any teeth. Minister: "On the judgment day, teeth will be provided."

594. Doctor: "Weak eyes, have you? Well, how many lines can you read on this chart?" Patient: "What chart?"

595. A man, in seeking admission for his son, told the Dean that his son was a follower who got along well with others. The Dean replied: "Send him along; we already have 988 leaders and we need one follower."

596. Officer, to driver: "Wouldn't it help if you wiped off your windshield?" Driver: "I don't think so; I left my glasses at home."

597. A burglar broke into the Sheriff's office and stole his glasses. The Sheriff issued an all-points bulletin: "Be on the lookout for a dark gray blob!"

598. Harry's wife knows he is good to his employees. When he is asleep and dreaming, he says things like: "I'll see you and raise you fifty dollars."

599. One of the benefits of the automotive age is that it's practically stopped horse stealing.

600. Maternity is a matter of fact; paternity is always a matter of opinion. J.C. Ridpath.

601. Two great things about Alzheimer's disease: You get to hide your own Easter eggs and you make new friends every day.

602. Wife to husband coming in at 2 A.M.: "Where have you been?" Husband: "Playing golf." Wife: "After dark?" Husband: "We were using night clubs."

603. Lady on witness stand, to cross-examining attorney in a bastardy proceeding: "What do you think I am?" The Attorney: "We've already established that: now, we're trying to determine the degree."

604. House buyer, complaining to Realtor: "There was a washing machine in the house when we moved in , but it isn't working too good. Last week, I put fourteen shirts in it, pulled the chain, and I haven't seen any of the shirts since."

605. When you are kicked from the rear, it means that you're in front.

606. Gracie Burns had to rush home from the studio set because her sister just had a baby. W.C. Fields: "Was it a boy or a girl?" Gracie: "I don't know; that's why I have to rush home—to find out whether I'm an uncle or an aunt."

607. George Burns: "To me, genius is 1% inspiration and 99% good writers."

608. "How do you sculpture an elephant?" "You take a block of marble and chip away anything that doesn't look like an elephant."

609. Lady in presence of her small son to waitress: "May I have a bag to take leftovers to my dog?" Son: "Oh, mother, are we going to get a dog?"

610. Love your enemies in case your friends turn out to be a bunch of bastards.

611. I take my children everywhere but they always find their way back home. Robert Orbin.

612. A British mother's advice to her daughter on how to survive the wedding night: "Close your eyes and think of England."

613. If homosexuality were normal, God would have created Adam and Bruce. Anita Bryant.

614. There's a great woman behind every idiot. John Lennon.

615. There is no gravity; the earth sucks. Gravitto.

616. Tommy Cooper: "Last night I dreamed I ate a ten-pound marshmallow; and when I awoke, the pillow was gone."

617. Jimmy Stewart: "After age seventy, it's just patch, patch, patch."

618. The family that eats together gets fat.

619. What good is gossip if you can't repeat it?

620. Be reasonable, do it my way.

621. Since I gave up hope, I feel much better.

622. Famous last words: "Trust me, I'm a doctor!"

623. The difference between the Polish Mafia and the Italian Mafia is that the Italian Mafia makes you an offer you can't refuse and the Polish Mafia makes you an offer you can't understand.

624. An oral agreement is not worth the paper it's written on.

625. What is Italian matched crystal? Answer: Three empty jars of the same brand of peanut butter.

626. A blind sky diver had to give up the sport because it was too hard on his seeing eye dog.

627. Research scientists are considering substituting lawyers for the white rats they use in their experiments because they are more numerous and the researches don't tend to get as attached to them.

628. A lady was introduced as being listed in Who's Who in the Midwest, Who's Who in America, and Who's Who of American Woman by an emcee who boasted that he was listed in Who's That?

629. Iowa has just passed a law requiring all car dimmer switches to be mounted on the floor because they found that the drivers were getting their feet tangled up in the steering wheels.

630. I now have 180 books but no book case; no one will loan me a bookcase.

631. I thought I was wrong but I was mistaken.

632. In applying for a job, where it asked the woman her age, one woman put down: "Nuclear."

633. Instead of spending all that money on bombs, we should just get the enemy to stand closer together.

634. An old maid spent 3 days at the airport getting frisked—what was so surprising was that she didn't even have a ticket.

635. A golfer got caught in a hurricane and made a hole in none.

636. I have no objection to snow falling. What I object to is me falling.

637. While a farmer went overseas with the army, his girlfriend met another boyfriend, so she wrote the farmer a John Deere letter.

638. Chairman, presiding at a meeting: "Is there a jockey in the house? I want someone to ride that fellow out of here."

639. It takes at least 48 rabbits to make a sealskin coat.

640 One woman wanted to see something in a fur so her husband took her to the zoo.

641. One Beverly Hills kid won a prize for having the most parents at a PTA meeting.

642. If God were Howard Cosell, Moses would have had to send down for more tablets.

643. He carries pictures of his children and a sound track of his wife.

644. A leading actor in a play was surprised when the telephone on stage rang at the wrong time. Nonplussed, he picked up the receiver, turned to his co-star and said: "It's for you."

645. I want to send my brother-in-law a present. How do you gift wrap a saloon?

646. He doesn't drive his car; he aims it.

647. Consideration is being given to renaming our nearest satellite the TRUMP, formerly the moon.

648. Newspaper ad: "Wanted—man to understudy human cannon ball; must be willing to travel."

649. W.C. Fields: "Women are like elephants to me: I like to look at them but I wouldn't want to own one."

650. Once, I threw myself on the mercy of the Court, and missed.

651. Half the world doesn't know how the other half lives, but is trying to find out. E.W. Howe.

652. Attributed to U.S. Grant during a visit in 1879: "Venice would be a fine city if it were only drained."

653. While I do enjoy lamb chops alone, I would much prefer to have a friend for dinner.
Dr. Hannibal Lecter.

654. Kirk Douglas, while in Norway making a movie, asked a young man if it ever stopped raining. The young man's reply: "I don't know, I'm only 18."

655. A Hollywood mogul has built a new house that's in 4 area codes.

656. Occasionally, I like to think deep thoughts—like: "What does Robert Schuller say when he stubs his toe?"

657. Question—how do you make antifreeze?
Answer—you steal her blanket.

658. A sweater is something you put on when your mother is cold.

659. Christmas is the season when a lot of people come unglued trying to wrap things up.

660. An autobiography is the life story of an automobile.

661. A minister left his church because of illness. His congregation got sick of him.

662. Horace: "That man is either crazy or he is a poet."

663. Attributed to Leo Durocher: "Show me a good loser and I'll show you an idiot."

664. While making a cowboy movie with John Wayne, Kirk Douglas learned how to do trick mounts using a trampoline. When somebody told Wayne how handy Kirk was with the horse, Wayne snorted: "He can't even get on (a horse) unless he uses a trampoline."

665. A Norwegian had his brain removed for examination. When he didn't return for 2 years, it was discovered that he had been away teaching in Sweden.

666. If your enemy wrongs you, buy each of his children a drum.

667. "I have 4 aces." "You win; I only have 3 aces."

668. Meditation: "It's not what you think."

669. Said to a small person: "Good things come in small packages." Small person's rejoinder: "So does poison."

670. Peak performers keep their eyes open so that when they get to the top of the ladder, they do not find that it's against the wrong wall.

671. A familiar saying in the French foreign legion: "When in doubt, gallop."

672. A black man tried unsuccessfully a number of times to join a Southern Baptist church. The minister asked him why he quit trying. The black man said that he talked it over with God, and God said not to feel bad, that he himself had been trying to get in for 30 years.

673. Larry King, hospitalized with a heart condition, was visited by a long-time friend who told of lying in bed with his wife when she asked: "Do you love me most of anyone in the whole world," to which the friend replied very casually, "Well, I love you a whole lot; I think you would be number four."

674. He had a winning smile but everything else was a loser. (George Scott at a Bob Hope roast.)

675. You are getting old when you get winded playing checkers or you sink your teeth into a steak and they stay there.

676. "Progress might have been alright once but it has gone on too long." Ogden Nash.

677. Impossible challenge: to eat only one salted peanut.

678. Groucho Marx: "Military intelligence is a contradiction in terms."

679. The toughest part of dieting isn't watching what you eat, it's watching what your friends eat.

680. Dennis the Menace, to his mother: "Mr. Wilson is cleaning the trash out of his garage and I was the first to go."

681. Ziggy, getting some pills from his psychiatrist: "And if these pills make you feel too euphoric, tune in the news."

682. Lady Violet Carter: "Outer space is no place for a person of breeding."

683. On being told in 1933 that Calvin Coolidge had died, Dorothy Parker asked: "How can they tell?"

684. A Minneapolis business man, in seeking to make peace between Minneapolis and St. Paul proposed that the names be combined to Minnehaha—Minne for Minneapolis and haha for St. Paul.

685. The last thing that the Tanzanians do at a wedding is to flush the punchbowl.

686. Definition of a gentleman farmer: One who has more hay in the bank than in the barn.

687. Will Rogers formula for preventing wars: move the countries around. Have France change places with Mexico, etc. Swap Canada with Ireland—but don't tell the English.

688. In the Winfield, Kansas, *Courier:* "As an encore, Mrs. Brown played the old favorite: 'Carry Me Back to Old Virginity.'"

689. W.C. Fields: "I am free of all prejudice, I hate everybody equally."

690. A mechanical klutz said: "I recently bought my first VCR and accidentally plugged it into our microwave; I watched the "Winds of War" in 6 minutes.

691. A man in a balloon is lost, hollers down to a man on the ground: "Where are we?" Man on the ground replies: "You are in a balloon." The balloonist says to his companion: "That must be a lawyer. He speaks with authority, talks directly to the point, and conveys no information."

692. A doctor gave his patient six months to live; when he had not paid his bill in that time, he gave him another six months.

693. Doctor to patient: "If you can't afford the operation, I'll just touch up the X-ray."

694. Will Rogers proposed to solve the U Boat menace during World War I by boiling the ocean. When asked how to do that, he replied: "That's your problem; I'm just the idea man."

695. Exasperated man to his computer: "Do you understand the meaning of the word 'sledgehammer'?"

696. A man caught a fish that was so big that the picture of it alone weighed 12 pounds.

697. A man to his slow moving cab driver: "Can't you go any faster?" His answer: "Yes, but I have to stay with the cab."

698. An Indian girl married a Jewish boy. To please their unhappy parents, they name their first child WHITEFISH.

699. A regular customer on Western Airlines, when asked by the stewardess what he wanted to drink, replied: "I'll just have what the pilot is drinking."

700. An old timer reported that, in his barnstorming days, he used to drop his sister's paper to her from his plane. He said that if he tried that today in one of the modern planes, the paper would probably land in England.

701. A New York society club advised Robert Benchley that he could not resign because he had already been suspended for non-payment of dues.

702. Yogi Berra said that his team lost the game because they made the wrong mistakes.

703. To err is human but it feels divine.

704. God save us from a bad neighbor and from a beginner on the trombone.

705. A Southern church struck oil on its property so they voted to close the membership roles.

706. She runs the gamut of emotions, all the way from A to B. Dorothy Parker.

707. Eternity is a terrible thought; I mean, where is it going to end?

708. G.B. Shaw: "If all the economists were laid end to end, they still would not reach a conclusion."

709. People who keep dogs are cowards who haven't got the courage to bite people themselves.

710. W.C. Fields: "I did not say that this meat was tough. I just said that I didn't see the horse that usually stands outside."

711. Ziggy, to his veterinarian about his pet duck: "He's lost his will to waddle."

712. Ben Franklin: "Fish and visitors smell after 3 days."

713. Christopher Fry: "What, after all, is a halo? It's only one more thing to keep clean."

714. Will Rogers: "Live your life so that whenever you lose, you are ahead."

715. When Will Rogers was in Europe, he said he didn't visit Queen Marie of Romania because he couldn't find the country.

716. A man's pajamas were so worn that when he sat down with a dime in the pocket, he could tell whether it was heads or tails.

717. Robert Benchley book: "Success with Small Fruits." College courses he studied: "History of Lace Making," "Russian Taxation Systems before Catherine the Great," "North American Glacial Deposits," and "Early Renaissance Etchers."

718. Morris Udall, referring to former Democratic Committee Chairman Robert Strauss: "He can follow you through a revolving door and come out first."

719. Benchley: "I don't think it is generally known that most of our boys (at a certain camp) are between the ages of 14."

720. Byron: "Life is too short for chess."

721. A comic situation: "A man in prison striped garb goes up to a policeman to ask directions."

722. Karate is one of the oldest forms of defense but it's not as good as running.

723. Writer Barbara Ehrenrench, of New York, upon dropping everything to get home to see a TV special: "I left my exercise class after I'd done only one leg; I risked asymmetry."

724. The first thing that strikes a stranger in New York is a big car.

725. A man is lining up a coat for his Great Dane dog and, in talking to the fitter, the fitter asks: "Is the dog expected to grow?"

726. Automobile: a guided missile.

727. George Fisher: "When you aim for perfection, you discover that it's a moving target.

728. Teacher: "Who was sorry when the prodigal son returned home?" Student: "The fatted calf."

729. The oboe is an ill wind that nobody plays good.

730. Instead of spending all that money on bombs, we should just get the enemy to stand closer together.

731. Stanley Baldwin: "One could not even dignify him with the name of stuffed shirt; he was simply a hole in the air."

732. Ross MacDonald: "There's nothing wrong with Southern California that a rise in the ocean level wouldn't cure."

733. When people complained to Thomas Edison about how hard it was to open his front gate, he explained that each time they did so, they pumped a gallon of water into the water tank on the roof.

734. Former baseball manager Chuck Tanner: "He's so optimistic that he'd buy a burial suit with two pairs of pants."

735. Consistency requires you to be as ignorant today as you were a year ago. Bernard Berman.

736. A man has developed a case of reverse paranoia. He imagines that he is following people.

737. Ben Franklin: "It's better to give than to lend and it costs about the same."

738. If you don't like the way I drive, stay off the sidewalk.

739. When Mrs. Glinski asked her husband if he would help straighten up the house, he replied: "Why? Is it tilted?"

740. Minnesota: where the elite meet the sleet.

741. Parishioner to new Pastor as she was leaving the service: I must say, we parishioners didn't even know what sin was until you took charge of our parish.

742. A young terrorist was sent to blow up a car. In trying to do so, he burnt his lips on the tail pipe.

743. Father to son: "You've got to set a goal and never quit. Remember George Washington?" "Yes" "Abraham Lincoln?" "Yes" "Azador McIngle?" "No, who was he?" Father: "See, you don't remember him. He quit."

744. A man can wait 3 hours for a fish to bite who can't wait 5 minutes for dinner.

745. Minnesota: Many are cold but few are frozen, or "Have you jump started your child lately?"

746. A man who was considering joining a church, upon his arrival at the service, heard the minister reading from the Apostle Paul: "We have left undone those things we ought to have done and done those things we ought not to have done" and commented to the minister gratefully, as he was leaving the church: "At last, I have found my kind of people."

747. After an elephant and a flea had crossed a bridge together, the flea said to the elephant: "Boy, did we shake that thing."

748. A minister had 4 Sunday school children each wear a letter in the word "Star," being the subject on which he was preaching. In turning around to face the congregation, the children got out of order and spelled the word "Rats."

749. A man read that women live to age 78 on average whereas men only live to age 72, so he plans to have a sex change operation as soon as he reaches age 71.

750. People who live in stone houses shouldn't throw glasses.

751. Tourist to Indian: "How big a fire do you make when you send smoke signals?" Indian: "A small fire for local calls and a big one for long distance calls."

752. Boss to new job applicant: "For a man with no experience, you certainly ask high wages." Job applicant: "Yes, but it's much harder to work when you don't know what you're doing."

753. A friend is someone who dislikes the same people you do.

754. A Russian named Rudolph looked out the window and told his wife it was raining. She replied: "No, it sleeting." "It's raining", he persisted, "Rudolph the red knows rain, dear."

755. John Paul Jones, in his battle with the British frigate declared "We have not yet begun to fight" just as one of his Swedish sailors, who was badly battered and mangled, emerged on deck and exclaimed: "There's always some dumb guy who doesn't get the word."

756. Bob Hope, in dedicating the new Disney Theme Park in Florida: "It's the largest such park in the world run by its actors and cartoon characters, unless you want to count Washington, DC."

757. Will Rogers kidded President Wilson on the peace negotiations, saying: "Do you people realize that at one point in the negotiations, President Wilson was 5 notes behind."

758. Will Rogers said, in addressing a group of farmers: "Farmers, I am proud to report that the country as a whole is prosperous. I don't mean by that that the whole country is prosperous, but as a hole it is prosperous. That is, it is prosperous as a hole. A hole is not supposed to be prosperous and you are certainly in a hole."

759. People who think they know it all really annoy those of us who do.

760. Small child to father: "Are we having fun yet?"

761. It's no use waiting for your ship to come in if you don't have one out.

762. Wilson Mizner: "If that radio announcer doesn't get off the air, I'll stop breathing it."

763. Since the earth's surface is ¼ land and ¾ water, it's obvious that we were intended to spend ¾ of our time fishing.

764. In one church, the minister preached on the text: "Launch Into The Deep" after which the choir sang the well-known hymn: "Pull for the Shore."

765. Gracie Burns believed that by shortening the vacuum cleaner cord she could save on the electric bill.

766. She said that her favorite musical instrument was the baton.

767. She is reported to have thrown a flute away because it had holes in it.

768. George Burns reported that Gracie had a relative who collected pendulum clocks. He once stayed there for a week and never got any sleep.

769. One good turn gets most of the blanket.

770. A reporter once asked Robert Benchley for a list of the 10 "most" people in the world. He replied that he could only name the 10 "least."

771. Benchley, again: "At the Camp, we needed to get the furnace repaired and let it out for bids with the understanding that if they were not hired, we should pay them nothing for submitting the bids. This clause alone saved us a great deal of money."

772. Gracie Burns had a nephew who got a terrible cold. The doctor told him to take something warm so he took the doctor's overcoat.

773. A lady was endeavoring to cash a check at a bank. The cashier asked her if she had anything by which she could be identified. She replied: "I think so, yes; I have a wart on the back of my neck."

774. Typical question of student in 1965: "What's the capitol of Wyoming?" In 1975: "Where's Wyoming?" In 1985: "Where is the United States?" In 1995: "What planet are we on?"

775. A man in northern Minnesota by the name of Charlie shot a Loon and ate it for dinner. The local Game Warden, a friend, heard about this, and went to him saying "Charlie, you should know better than to shoot our state bird. It's illegal, and I'm going to have to fine you." After the warden fined Charlie $100, he said "Say, Charlie, just out of curiosity, what does a Loon taste like?" Charlie replied: It wasn't too bad, kind of a cross between a bald eagle and a trumpeter swan."

776. A mother, worried over the possible wear and tear on the family nerves from her son's first musical efforts, asked Sir Thomas Beecham which instrument he should take up, the violin or the trombone. He recommended bagpipes, saying that they sound the same when you have mastered them as when you first begin. (Sir Thomas was the famed British conductor.)

777. A certain boxer, being terribly beaten and mauled, in going to his corner after a round, said his opponent "never laid a glove on me." The trainer replied: "Well, you better keep an eye on the referee then, because somebody is beating the hell out of you."

778. Sandra Kurtzy, owner of a major computer company, in addressing a group of fellow executives, said: "When I started this company, my long-range planning consisted of figuring out where to have lunch." She also added that when she made a point in a speech that it reminded her speech writer of a joke.

779. A veterinarian and a taxidermist are considering merging their practices so that, either way, you get your pet back.

780. The earth's shell is composed of numerous plates from 45 to 95 miles thick, slowly migrating. A geologist calls the United States, "the United Plates of America." United only for now.

781. An advertising executive named Fred Hoar starts a speech by saying: "My name is Fred Hoar; that's spelled FRED."

782. Philosopher: "You should never finish something you haven't started."

783. Henny Youngman says he won't lend his brother-in-law money anymore because it gives him amnesia.

784. A fact: The average coffee tree yields 1½ pounds of coffee in a year. One speaker said that he knew of friends who drank a tree in a day.

785. An analogy used in a lawyer's closing argument: "Getting information out of Marie is like trying to suck a bowling ball through a 50-foot garden hose."

786. After making a presentation to a hostile audience, Joe DiMisci, Vice President of a computer company, said: "I feel like a friend of mine who had to ride his bike home after a vasectomy."

787. When a husband said he couldn't think of anything to say to his mother-in-law, his wife replied: "Don't gimme that; there are hundreds of things you could apologize for."

788. If you feel awed by people you encounter, just visualize them as being dressed in red woolen underwear.

789. A diplomat is a person who can tell you to go to hell in such a way that you actually look forward to the trip. Caskie Stinnett.

790. Former Chrysler President Cafiero traveled to England to meet workers at a troubled plant there. One worker challenged him, saying: "I'm Eddie McClusky and I'm a communist." Cafiero extended his hand and said: "How do you do; I'm Eugene Cafiero and I'm a Presbyterian."

791. FDR revealed his secrets of public speaking: "Be sincere, be brief, be seated."

792. Former Vice President Bush, in a speech coupling himself with President Reagan, made an error, saying: "We've had triumphs; we've made mistakes; we've had sex." (He meant "setbacks.") When the laughter had subsided, he said: "I feel like the javelin thrower who won the toss and elected to receive."

793. A waiter who goofed up an order said, "I'm terribly sorry; my memory is good—it's just short."

794. The President of Disney corporation, Michael Eisner, was asked what his favorite ride is. His answer: "The stock market."

795. George Will: "An earthquake is a tough teacher but it tells the truth."

796. Paderewski, the famed Polish pianist and statesman, was accompanying a very poor soloist. When he played the high notes she would sing the low, etc. Finally, in disgust, he stood and exclaimed: "Lady, I've played on the white notes and I've played on the black notes, but always you sing on the cracks."

797. Nurse, to husband visiting his sick wife: "Don't worry, we'll have her up and shopping in no time."

798. The two biggest sellers in any book store are the cookbooks and the diet books. The cookbooks tell you how to prepare the food and the diet books tell you how not to eat any of it.

799. There are three classes of people in the world: Those who make things happen, those who watch things happen and those who wonder what happened.

800. Two Nevada Indian chiefs were arguing over territorial rights to an atomic test sight when an atomic blast occurred. A giant mushroom cloud appeared. One of the chiefs looked at it and thought: "I wish I'd said that."

801. Louis Brandeis: "Sunlight is the best of all disinfectants."

HENRY W. HAVERSTOCK, JR.

by Robert T. Smith

It was a Sunday in the autumn of 1939. For some reason it happened a lot during the fall of the year.

Henry W. Haverstock, Jr., then an active seventeen-year-old youth who played sandlot football and pole vaulted and, with his father, hunted and fished, was putting a golf ball in his back yard. He had dug holes in the lawn, and was having fun trying to get the white ball into them. At one point, he knelt down to retrieve the ball from a hole. He could not get up, at least not without help.

The incident came almost without warning. The previous day, however, he had awakened with a rather severe pain in his back and the back of his head. It had lasted about three hours, then had disappeared.

With effort, Henry finally got up from a kneeling to a standing position at his makeshift golf course, and continued the game. But he became weaker and weaker. With the aid of a brother, he made it inside the house to a couch. Then, again with help, he went to his bed. There he stayed for five months.

Henry, born in Minneapolis in 1922, went to Burroughs Elementary School, Ramsey Junior High and then Washburn Senior High School.

His lawyer father, a strong-minded but loving man, taught his son many things. Particularly, he taught young Henry that you do not give up, no matter what the adversity. The idea was to take problems and turn them into assets.

Young Henry had a normal childhood. He loved to be outdoors, to run and laugh and feel the strength mounting in his growing body. He believed, as most children do, that he was invincible, and immortal and that nothing bad could happen to him. And nothing untoward did happen to him until that autumn day in 1939.

After going from the couch to his bed, young Henry began to feel heavy pain. It affected his legs and abdomen and back; and his arms and hands. In the first week, his temperature got as high as 104 degrees. For three weeks, he could not move without agonizing pain. "So great was the pain," he remembers, "that all wrinkles in the sheets and buttons on the mattress had to be removed before I felt in the least degree comfortable."

For six weeks, he had no treatment. No one seemed to know for sure what he had, for at that time not much was known about polio. They even called it by a different name: infantile paralysis. It is a disease of the nerves, and it probably was best that during the first weeks of pain, Henry did not know what hit him.

After the first six weeks, treatment began. The seventeen-year-old wasn't bitter about his affliction. He figured he would give it a good fight. He began strenuous exercise and massage. He used a four-wheeled walker—a metal-framed cart with a seat in the center. He sat on it and made it go with his legs. He invented exercises on that cart, movements for his legs, back and abdominal muscles.

The exercises and massage treatments kept him busy from 10 a.m. to 8 p.m. He operated a rig consisting of a wooden board three-and-a-half feet long, with a roller skate on each end. "I would lie on my side with one leg on the skate rig, and move my leg back and forth as the rig rolled on a large table leaf," Haverstock remembers.

There were three hospital stays, and he wore full-length leg braces from February to June, 1940. There was some improvement. But that could well have been normal improvement noticed by many polio victims in the early months of the disease. It might have happened without the exercises and massages and casts.

It was Haverstock's senior year at Washburn when he contracted polio. He was the only kid in his class who got it, and he had to graduate in a wheelchair. But he did not seek pity and was rewarded in kind by his fellow students—they did not offer any pity. It was about this time that Haverstock learned to use his head more than most of his friends. "Thinking became my hobby."

In February, 1940, he traveled to Warm Springs, Georgia, the favorite spa of President Franklin Delano Roosevelt, himself a polio victim. "Warm Springs was beautiful. The buildings were pillared and white, and surrounded by rich green lawns." The medical staff at Warm Springs fitted Haverstock for braces— full-length leg splints, a body brace, even a thumb splint. He was put to bed for four months, getting out only once in the morning for exercise in the special pool and a light massage.

But instead of concentrating on the muscles which might make him walk again, the staff members had a coordinated muscle program. He could use other muscles to help his legs move. "In short, it was a failure," says Haverstock. "The muscles which should have been strengthened were weak, and gradually wasting away. The braces plus a body cast, served to stiffen my legs and torso."

After several weeks he was permitted to sit in a wheelchair for fifteen minutes a day, then twenty, then twenty-five. Finally, he was allowed to wheel himself around the complex at will.

He left Warm Springs June 3, 1940, a somewhat dejected youth. Among the last things they told him were: "No victim of polio who has paralysis ever regains full use of his muscles. You, Henry, will never be able to walk." They did not know Haverstock very well. "I have never thought of myself as a cripple."

His father drove him home from Georgia. Young Haverstock lay on a stretcher settled across the two car seats. On the way, his father talked to him about how there would be no such thing as quitting the fight against the disease. When they arrived home, Henry was put to bed in his leg braces and body cast. He was not, of course, able to stand or walk.

Then came Sister Elizabeth Kenny. The tough, outspoken backlander from Australia, who bullied doctors and snorted at the then-current treatments for polio, became the means for a young high school graduate to realize his goal. Haverstock became Sister Kenny's first regular patient in this country. When the formidable woman originally met with the young man, she said, "You'll walk."

"I believed her," said Haverstock. Then Sister Kenny looked him over, and ordered the braces off. "I never want to see them again."

Haverstock remembers well that first encounter with the remarkable woman: "My feeling toward her as she slowly stepped into my bedroom at home was one of awe and respect. She bore herself erectly. Her appearance was that of one who had been called upon to shoulder all the troubles of a war-torn world. Her face was serious and she looked deeply thoughtful. I greeted her with a cheerful 'Good morning,' which she promptly returned."

Henry's father carried him downstairs and placed him on the dining room table, at Sister Kenny's request. She then examined Haverstock more carefully. With a bit of humor, Haverstock comments, "I then knew where the phrase, she was 'Peck-peck-pecking all around' originated in the popular 1940 song hit."

There followed the famous Kenny treatment, which included training him to know the location and function of his various muscles. A year later, young Haverstock was walking with the aid of crutches. "The nurses couldn't believe their eyes," he remembers.

With his crutches and his sense of humor, Haverstock began life in a world designed for the non-handicapped. The world came in second.

He entered the University of Minnesota and discovered that, for some perverse reason, most of his classes were on upper floors. He made the stairs daily by keeping close to the walls. "And the steps outside the buildings were a terror, particularly in the winter." With the help of special equipment, he could drive a car, which made his life more comfortable.

As in high school, the University students did not cause Haverstock any trouble. No pity or teasing. "I had help, if anything." But he became somewhat of a loner. It helped with his contemplation, aided in the development of his thinking process. "I found being somewhat of a loner a virtue," he says. "I did not mind being a majority of one."

Haverstock graduated from the University in 1945 and went to the University of Southern California, where a year later he received a law degree. Then began an impressive career in law and service to his community, and a full life as a husband and father. The following are just some of his activities and accomplishments:

First chairman, Architectural Barriers Committee of the Minnesota Society for Crippled Children and Adults, now Courage Center; chairman, Minnesota State Bar Association Special Committee to codify and redraft the Minnesota State Criminal Code; chairman four years and director twenty-two years, of the Minneapolis Downtown YMCA; past president, Metropolitan YMCA Men's Club; past president, Minneapolis Downtown Exchange Club.

Selected by *Time* Magazine and the Minneapolis Chamber of Commerce as one of 100 Outstanding Young Men in 1953.

Past chairman, Minnesota State Bar Association committee which created the KSTP-Radio series, "You and the Law"; former instructor, William Mitchell College of Law; for twenty years a member of the speakers bureau of the Community Chest, now the United Way.

Politically, this "handicapped" man has been very active. He was a delegate to many county and state Republican conventions in Minnesota, and was formerly chairman of the research committee of the Hennepin County Young Republican League. In 1956 he ran, unsuccessfully, for the Republican nomination for Minnesota attorney general.

Haverstock has worked long and hard to improve things for the handicapped in Minnesota. Besides serving on the board of Courage Center for many years, he has spent time lobbying with local and state governments.

With his help, Minnesota became one of the first states in the nation to adopt a comprehensive legal code requiring such things as ramps and slanted curbing for those in wheelchairs. "People should spend a day in a wheelchair," said Haverstock. Then we'd get a lot of action. "

He considers the Minneapolis Skyway system a model of architecture for the handicapped. Referring to the Investors' Diversified Services Company, he says, "We got IDS to spend $40,000 just to eliminate four steps to the Skyway. It's a ramp now."

Not everything has gone well, though. Haverstock is perplexed by one Minneapolis area shopping center. Wanting to do things right in terms of the handicapped, the center's designer put ramps in everywhere. "Then they constructed a raised, decorative section between the handicapped parking spaces and the front door. It had curbs all around it, hindering wheelchair access."

Haverstock was married to his first wife, Jean, in 1950. They had three children, Henry W. III; William W. "Bill"; and Alice. Jean died at age forty-nine of cancer. In 1970, Haverstock married his present wife, Shirley, who has one daughter, Patricia.

In recent years, aside from his Minneapolis law practice, Haverstock has had a "hobby": real estate. He has bought more than fifty properties, including office and apartment buildings; and farm land. He is now working on a book about his real estate dealings entitled, *Wealth From a Wheelchair.*

The "wheelchair" of that title reflects his life since 1977. He walked with only the crutches for thirty-seven years, but it took its toll on his knees. The knee muscles finally gave out, and he now gets around in a wheelchair. But even in that he finds good. "With the crutches, I used to be terrified by winter icy conditions. I'm not at all worried now in a wheelchair."

When he is not in court or making a real estate deal or working for some community cause, Haverstock indulges in his hobbies: wood carving, rug hooking, stamp collecting and traveling. "We've gone just about everywhere, including a trip around the world." And he reads, everything from the *Wall Street Journal* to non-fiction books such as *Future Shock.*

Haverstock has used his sense of humor well to help him in life. He can tell jokes or relate humorous experiences he has had. Part of it is to get by situations involving people who are uncomfortable around the handicapped.

"I like to talk to people, at parties and such. But some ignore you if you are in a wheelchair. I've gotten used to it, but sometimes it makes me angry. It bothers me that people can't deal with realities."

And Haverstock has another little pet peeve. Some people tend to hover over him when conversing. "It gives you the feeling people are looking down at you." It is better when they sit down and the person in a wheelchair can look them in the face instead of at their stomachs.

Then there are those who think, if you are in a wheelchair, you are mentally deficient. Haverstock, for instance, is not pleased when waiters or waitresses automatically hand the bill to his wife.

And what is the philosophy of this man who was cut down by polio at the age of seventeen?

First of all, he agrees with Abraham Lincoln: "You are as happy as you make up your mind to be." Nothing magical from the outside is going to make you happy, if you have made up your mind to be bitter.

Is he better off because he had polio? He thinks so. "Without the experiences that came with polio, I think I would not have developed as much mentally. I'd have made a living, I guess, but maybe not have done as many things in life."

As he says, thinking is his main hobby. "I like to puzzle things out." And he's not past oriented, as he claims ninety-five per cent of people are. "I like to know where I'm going and how to use what I know to get there. The hard part is to figure out where one wants to go.

"Too many people are shackled with rigidities and complexes. . . . We need flexibility in life.

"A lot of people are stuck in the mud, going nowhere fast."

But not Henry W. Haverstock, Jr., whose only crutches in life were made in Canada.

The preceding biography was written by Robert T. Smith and appeared in the book *Tributes to Courage*, published by Courage Center, Golden Valley, Minnesota, and reprinted here with their permission.

Robert T. Smith, columnist for the Minneapolis Tribune, specializes in people and human experiences. In his twenty some years in journalism, he has covered beats ranging from the neighborhood police station all the way to President Charles de Gaulle of France.

Born in Minneapolis, Smith attended the College of St. Thomas in St. Paul and was graduated from the University of Minnesota. An ensign in the United States Navy during World War II, he spent his six final months of active duty in north China.

Smith is former City Editor of the Minneapolis *Tribune*. During the Kennedy administration he was News Editor of *Time* Magazine's Washington Bureau. For five years he was Deputy Bureau Chief for *Time* in Paris.

JUST A MOMENT, PLEASE
AH...WELL... A MOMENT OR TWO

OR THREE...
OR FOUR...
OR FIVE...
OR SIX
OR SEVEN
OR EIGHT

OR, OR, OR

"COMPUTERS" *&%^$%#$%%^@%^&

Henry! Be nice! Tell the readers to turn the page.

You Can Tell Your Own One-Liners

When you focus attention on the daily world around you at home, office, and even in shopping centers and at school, you can often see humorous situations and hear funny one-liners from the actual conversations. The problem is trying to remember them even when you repeat them several times to friends and family.

The answer is to write the words down carefully so you can actually repeat them months later. One-liners seem to change as you tell them to others, a word here, a phrase there, and you have a different statement... sometimes no longer funny. Try to keep the situation first seen and heard described simply in the words written. Jokes and humor often happen spontaneously. Don't trust yourself to remember without recording the words.

The following pages have been prepared to be a place for some of your own funny one-liners to be permanently kept for future fun. Write them on the pages clearly in ink. And remember, the funniest one-liners are based upon real situations exaggerated or viewed in an odd way combined with statements that might be heard in daily life.

Example: A (certain politician) promised the voters that, if elected, he would give them the best performance that money could buy.

Example: Announcer: Tonight I would like to present Mr. (you fill in name) , of whom the President of the United States said: "Who?"

Example: A _(Kurd, Irishman, etc.)_, won his country's equivalent of a million dollar lottery. He gets a dollar a year for a million years.

Humorous References

Kushner, Malcolm. 1990. *The Light Touch. How To Use Humor for Business Success*, New York: Simon and Schuster.

McLellan, Vern. 1988. *Shredded Wit*, Eugene, Oregon: Harvest House Publishers.

Rosen, Milton. 1985. *The Second Book of Insults*, New York: Pinnacle Books, Inc.

Orben, Robert. 1976, 1977, 1978, 1979, 1980, 1981, 1984. *2400 Jokes to Brighten Your Speeches*, New York: Doubleday & Company, Inc.

Youngman, Henny. 1984. *Take This Book Please*, New York: Gramercy Publishing Company. Dist. by Crown Publishers, Inc.

Bonham, Tal D. 1981. *The Treasury of Clean Jokes*, Broadman Press.

Strangland, Red. 1979. *Norwegian Jokes, Red Strangland's Original Book of*. Sioux Falls, SD: Norse Press.

Adams, Joey. 1978. *Joey Adams Joke Diary: Strictly for Laughs*, New York: Manor Books, Inc.

Youngman, Henny. 1978. *Insults for Everyone*, New York: Manor Books, Inc.

Manchester, Richard B. 1977. *The Mammoth Book of Fun and Games*, New York: Hart Publishing Company, Inc.

Peterson, Roland. 1976. *The Good Humor Book*, Santa Ana, CA: Vision House Publishers.

Phillips, Bob. 1976. *The All American Joke Book*, compiled by Harvest House Publishers.

Wilde, Larry. 1975. *The Official Italian Joke Book; The Official Polish Joke Book,* Pinnacle Books, Inc.

Phillips, Bob. 1974. *The Last of the Good Clean Joke Books,* Irvine, CA: compiled by Harvest House Publishers.

Phillips, Bob. 1974. *The World's Greatest Collection of Clean Jokes,* Santa Ana, CA: Vision House Publishers.

Schafer, Kermit. 1973. *Bloopers Bloopers Bloopers,* New York: Bell Publishing Company. Distributed by Crown Publishers, Inc. Copyright by Blooper Enterprises, Inc., a division of Kermit Schafer Productions.

1971. *The Wit and Wisdom of Archie Bunker,* Tandon Productions, Inc.

Owens, Jim. 1970. *Hillbilly Humor,* New York: Pocket Books, a division of Simon & Schuster.

Youngman, Henny. 1970. *Henny Youngman's Greatest One-liners,* New York: Pocket Books, a division of Simon & Schuster.

Marx, Groucho. 1967. *The Groucho Letters,* New York: Manor Books, Inc.

Murdock, Clyde. 1967. *A Treasury of Humor,* Grand Rapids, MI: Pyramid Publications for Zonderian Publishing House.

Copeland, Lewis and Faye. 1939, 1940, 1965. *10,000 Jokes, Jests and Stories* (a new revised edition of the world's largest collection), Garden City, New York: Doubleday & Company, Inc.

Marx, Groucho. 1963. *Memoirs of a Mangy Lover,* New York: Manor Books, Inc.

Twain, Mark. 1961. *Mark Twain Wit and Wisecracks,* Mount Vernon, NY: Peter Pauper Press and Harper & Brothers.

Prochnow, Herbert V. 1960. *The Complete Toastmaster,* Engelwood Cliffs, NJ: Prentice Hall, Inc.

Cerf, Bennett. 1959. *The Laugh's On Me,* New York: Pocket Books, Inc. Copyright by Bennett Cerf Illustrations.

Whiting, Percy H. 1959. *How To Speak and Write With Humor,* New York, Toronto, London: McGraw-Hill Book Company, Inc.

Brant House. 1958. *Lincoln's Wit,* Copyright by Ace Books, Inc., Collected and edited by Brant House.

Lindquist, I.S. (Mox). 1958. *A Collection of Minnesota Folklore and Scandinavian Stories,* E. C. Boynton Printing Co.

Golden, Francis Leo. 1950. *Laughter is Legal,* Frederick Fell, Inc. Published in the U.S. by Pocket Books, Inc.

Prochnow, Herbert V. 1942. *The Public Speaker's Treasure Chest,* New York and London: Harper & Brothers Publishers.

Fields, W.C. 1939, 1940. *Fields For President,* New York: Dodd, Mead & Co., Inc. and New York: Dell Publishing Co.

YOU MIGHT BECOME PUBLISHED!

One-liners and humorous short tales that can make people laugh and be happy in this difficult and stress-filled world are heard locally in towns and cities everywhere, but often the best one-liners soon are lost to the rest of the world. You can help change that and get credit, too, for original one-liners.

Henry's Publishing Company is interested in exposing more people, especially office workers and business people, to the joys of a little chuckle or a hearty laugh to offset the serious side of daily business.

Send your ORIGINAL one-liners and jokes, heard or experienced by you, your family and friends to us at the address below, typed or printed very clearly. If we think it is funny, too, we will consider including it in a future one-liner book crediting your name, city, and state. No One-liners Will Be Returned and They Become The Property of Henry's Publishing Company, Inc. to be used solely at its discretion. Include your full name, address, and age (Those eighteen or younger, please ask one of your parents to sign a copy of the statement below).

Please, do not use one-liners from newspapers, magazines, or other printed matter. Those one-liners heard on radio or television originally should list the show, date, station, and people identified and involved. Do not send any one-liners or jokes heard on humor shows or specials.

Include this statement, signed and dated:

> "I hereby give permission for my enclosed original one-liner and/or joke to be used by Henry's Publishing Company, Minneapolis, MN 55343, in any form, and release all rights to said company without payment." ______________________
>
> Your signature and date here.

Mail To: New One-liners, Henry's Publishing Company, Inc.
Post Office Box 5175, Minneapolis, MN 55343

If we include your one-liner, we will try to credit each author with a listing. No Guarantee, but wouldn't it be fun to be published in a book?!?

CLIPS, CARTOONS, AND QUIPS

The art of the joke as an important part of social interaction has slowly disappeared. Jokes are used mostly for entertainment on radio, television, and in professional publications; and often these are contrived and usually not as funny as those spontaneous situations and spoofs we do to each other in fun. Probably the decline in personal letter writing replaced by telephone talking is why jokes and one-liners are not recorded as often in written form, and people seem to be just more serious in their daily activities. Below I have listed the dictionary meanings for those parts of jokes and one-liners that can be developed from everyday experiences.

CLIPSHEETS (CLIPS)	-	*Sheets of newpaper stories, articles, and jokes to be saved. Usually placed on only one side of the paper.* Put them Up!
CARTOONS	-	*A drawing caricaturing some action or subject. A sequence of drawings relating to a comic incident or a story, often called a comic strip.* The best known of printed joke forms today, but usually produced professionally rather than by individuals for friends. At one time, many letters had one or more cartoons drawn in the margins by pen and colored inks.
QUIP(S)	-	*A clever or witty remark, usually sarcastic.* A quipster is the person who quips against others using verbal remarks.
CHUCKLING	-	*Softly laughing to oneself; Being amused.*
BELLY LAUGH	-	*A loud hearty laugh usually in an informal situation, but not always; and not required to have fun.*
ONE-LINER	-	*A brief, witty, or humorous remark, often written on more than one line, but spoken as if just in one continous form.*
HENRY'S ONELINERS	-	© copyrighted one-liners and jokes used in *Henry's Hilarious Oneliners* book and *Henry's Hilarious Postcards.*

You can find wonderful cartoons and short jokes in newspapers and a few magazines. Here is space to keep some of them. You may want to keep a file folder or 3-ring binder, too. Just dab a little glue on the backs and attach. Have lots of laughs at your fingertips!

"Man blames fate for other accidents, but feels personally responsible when he makes a hole-in-one." —HORIZONS

FAMILY HUMOROUS AND SHOCKING ONE-LINERS

One of the greatest sources of hilarious one-liners is your own family, especially young children who sometimes mix up new words resulting in very funny statements; and sadly these are the great moments that are forgotten unless recorded on video cameras or tape recorders. Below are spaces for you to record, carefully and clearly, the one-liners heard within your own family. Remember, don't wait! Write down the funny words just as heard on any available paper, then transcribe onto the pages in *Henry's Hilarious Oneliners* or another record book. Most people forget the one-liners very quickly—when the phone rings or a child calls out, or something else interferes with your short memory. You will enjoy, again and again, telling the funny experiences and repeating the one-liners. And, if you wish, send them in for potential publication.

A. ______________________________

____

____

B. ______________________________

____

____

C. ______________________________

____

____

D. ______________________________

____

____

E. ______________________________

____

____

FAMILY HUMOROUS ONE-LINERS

F.

G.

H.

I.

J.

K.

L.

M.

FAMILY SHOCKING ONE-LINERS

N. ____

O. ____

P. ____

Q. ____

R. ____

S. ____

T. ____

U. ____

FRIENDS' ONE-LINERS

V. ______________________________

____

____

Name ______________________________

W. ______________________________

____

____

Name ______________________________

X. ______________________________

____

____

Name ______________________________

Y. ______________________________

____

____

Name ______________________________

Z. ______________________________

____

____

Name ______________________________

I hope you have had lots of fun reading through HENRY'S HILARIOUS ONELINERS, and I know you will be re-reading them to catch all the funny ones you may have missed the first time through.

Don't forget to listen for all the funny things said every day that you can keep enjoying. And record those funny one-liners that happen every month in every family.

KEEP LAUGHING...

Henry of Hopkins

HI! JUST A FEW NOTES TO PASS ALONG...

SEND US YOUR ONE-LINER JOKES

MY FRIENDS HAVE PRINTED A FORM SHOWN ON THE NEXT PAGE FOR YOU TO USE. THEY HAVE GIVEN PERMISSION FOR YOU TO COPY FIVE OF THESE INDIVIDUAL FORMS IN ORDER TO MAIL YOUR ONE-LINERS TO HENRY'S PUBLISHING COMPANY.

DON'T FORGET TO SIGN AND DATE EACH FORM.

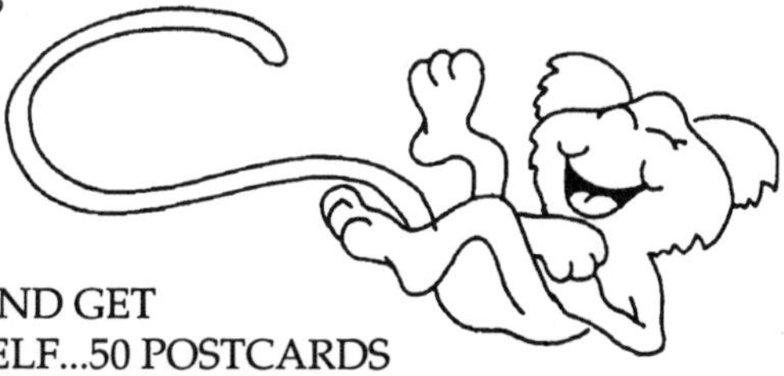

HENRY MY MAN IS PRINTING A NEAT PACKAGE OF HILARIOUS ONELINER POSTCARDS.
TELL EVERYONE AND GET THEM FOR YOURSELF...50 POSTCARDS PRINTED IN COLORFUL ALBUM FORM, WITH NEW ONE-LINERS, THE FUN ART AND CARTOONS FROM THIS BOOK, AND MORE CARTOONS!

MAKE YOUR FRIENDS LAUGH!
MAKE YOUR MOM & DAD LAUGH
SEND THEM TO STRANGERS AND YOU CAN LAUGH!

WE WILL GIVE SPECIAL DISCOUNTS FOR SOCIAL AND BUSINESS CLUBS ORDERING *HENRY'S HILARIOUS ONELINERS* AND *HENRY'S HILARIOUS POSTCARDS* FOR THEIR OWN INDIVIDUAL MEMBERS. SEND US A LETTER ON YOUR LETTERHEAD TO OUR PUBLISHER AT THE ADDRESS SHOWN. YOU MUST BE NON-PROFIT AND INCLUDE YOUR PROOF OF STATUS FOR EACH STATE OR FEDERAL TAX EXEMPT NUMBER. WE WILL SEND OUR SPECIAL ORDER FORM. A SOFTCOVER EDITION IS AVAILABLE. WE ARE BEING DISTRIBUTED NATIONALLY. LOCAL BOOKSTORES MAY REACH HENRY'S PUBLISHING COMPANY, INC. THROUGH P.O. BOX 5175, MINNEAPOLIS, MN 55343 OR CHECK WITH YOUR DISTRIBUTOR. HENRY'S PUBLISHING ISBN #1-879916; LISTED IN 1992 LMP and 1992 BOOKS IN PRINT, R.R. BOWKER. ADDITIONAL BOOKS AND PRODUCTS ARE BEING DEVELOPED FOR 1992.

Do not tear out this page—photocopy only.

TO HENRY OF HOPKINS, THE LAUGHING MOUSE™:
Here is my own original one-liner or joke. Please review it and, if possible, publish it in another book. I have signed the form below, or I had my parent sign because I am under eighteen years of age. Please let me know if it is accepted. I know I don't have to purchase a book to be included, and there is no guarantee at all. I may make up to five copies of this form to send in individual one-liners, one per page. All one-liners and letters become the property of Henry's Publishing Company.

"I, ______________________, hereby give permission for my enclosed one-liner or joke to be used by Henry's Publishing Company, Minneapolis, MN in any form, and release all rights to said company without payment."

PRINT/TYPE YOUR ONE-LINER:

____

____

____

____

____

______________________ ______________________

Date Signature

SENT BY:

____

____

____

____

Print Clearly in Ink or Type Mailing Name and Address. Phone Optional.

Place this form in an envelope to safeguard your one-liner. Mail with First-Class Stamp.

TO: *New One-Liner* Editor
Henry's Publishing Co.
Post Office Box 5175
Minneapolis, MN 55343-5175